ORCHARDS ORCHARDS ORCHARDS

Plays by

MARIA IRENE FORNES

SPALDING GRAY

JOHN GUARE

DAVID MAMET

WENDY WASSERSTEIN

MICHAEL WELLER

SAMM-ART WILLIAMS

BROADWAY PLAY PUBLISHING INC.

357 W 20th St., NY NY 10011
212 627-1055

ORCHARDS

Copyright © 1987 by Broadway Play Publishing, Inc.

For Maria Irene Fornes—Helen Merrill, 435 West 23 Street, New York, New York 10011

For Spalding Gray—Suzanne Gluck, ICM, 40 West 57 Street, New York, NY 10019

For John Guare—Andrew Boose, Kay Collyer Boose, 1 Dag Hammarskjold Plaza, New York, NY 10019

For David Mamet—Howard Rosenstone, 3 East 48 Street, New York, NY 10017

For Wendy Wasserstein—Arlene Donovan, ICM, 40 West 57 Street, New York, NY 10019

For Michael Weller—Howard Rosenstone, 3 East 48 Street, New York, NY 10017

For Samm-Art Williams—Broadway Play Publishing, Inc., 357 West 20 Street, New York, NY 10011

Original trade edition published by Alfred A. Knopf, Inc., 1986.

First printing: August 1987
ISBN: 0-88145-055-3

Manufactured in the United States of America on acid-free paper.

The seven plays in this book
were originally commissioned by
The Acting Company,
a national repertory theater
on tour for the John F. Kennedy Center

Producing Artistic Director
JOHN HOUSEMAN

Executive Producer
MARGOT HARLEY

Artistic Director
MICHAEL KAHN

"Commissioned" does not fully describe the unusual process through which the seven plays in this book were created.

The Acting Company, for which they were written, is the only permanent touring repertory ensemble in this country. Most of the fifty-nine plays it has performed in the past fifteen years in 298 American cities have been classics; because of the Company's traveling habits and insistence on repertory, it has had difficulty in attracting new plays, whose authors prefer to see them premiered in regular runs in New York or regional theaters.

In an attempt to find fresh contemporary material, the Company, under the stewardship of its Executive Producer, Margot Harley, came up with the notion of circulating a number of Chekhov's stories among a dozen of America's most successful young playwrights. The idea was not simply to adapt or dramatize the stories, but to use them as a cue for the creation of short theatrical pieces to be produced by the Company as part of its repertory season. The Company's dramaturg, Anne Cattaneo, read all of Chekhov's nearly one thousand stories and selected those she thought most compatible with the individual styles of the playwrights, whom she also selected.

Of the twelve writers approached, five declined, for valid personal or professional reasons; the rest came up with the variegated works contained in this volume. The plays have been rehearsed and presented by The Acting Company as part of its current tour. To date they have appeared in thirty-four cities, where in many cases audiences had their first opportunity to see works by the seven playwrights represented.

JOHN HOUSEMAN
New York, March 1986

CONTENTS

ORCHARDS

The Man in a Case

by

WENDY WASSERSTEIN

CHARACTERS

BYELINKOV

VARINKA

A small garden in the village of Mironitski. 1898.

BYELINKOV *is pacing. Enter* VARINKA *out of breath.*

BYELINKOV: You are ten minutes late.

VARINKA: The most amazing thing happened on my way over
here. You know the woman who runs the grocery store down
the road. She wears a black wig during the week, and a blond
wig on Saturday nights. And she has the daughter who married an engineer in Moscow who is doing very well thank you
and is living, God bless them, in a three-room apartment. But
he really is the most boring man in the world. All he talks
about is his future and his station in life. Well, she heard we
were to be married and she gave me this basket of apricots to
give to you.

BYELINKOV: That is a most amazing thing!

VARINKA: She said to me, Varinka, you are marrying the most
honorable man in the entire village. In this village he is the
only man fit to speak with my son-in-law.

BYELINKOV: I don't care for apricots. They give me hives.

VARINKA: I can return them. I'm sure if I told her they give you hives she would give me a basket of raisins or a cake.

BYELINKOV: I don't know this woman or her pompous son-in-law. Why would she give me her cakes?

VARINKA: She adores you!

BYELINKOV: She is emotionally loose.

VARINKA: She adores you by reputation. Everyone adores you by reputation. I tell everyone I am to marry Byelinkov, the finest teacher in the county.

BYELINKOV: You tell them this?

VARINKA: If they don't tell me first.

BYELINKOV: Pride can be an imperfect value.

VARINKA: It isn't pride. It is the truth. You are a great man!

BYELINKOV: I am the master of Greek and Latin at a local school at the end of the village of Mironitski.

(VARINKA *kisses him*)

VARINKA: And I am to be the master of Greek and Latin's wife!

BYELINKOV: Being married requires a great deal of responsibility. I hope I am able to provide you with all that a married man must properly provide a wife.

VARINKA: We will be very happy.

BYELINKOV: Happiness is for children. We are entering into a social contract, an amicable agreement to provide us with a secure and satisfying future.

VARINKA: You are so sweet! You are the sweetest man in the world!

BYELINKOV: I'm a man set in his ways who saw a chance to provide himself with a small challenge.

VARINKA: Look at you! Look at you! Your sweet round spectacles, your dear collar always starched, always raised, your perfectly pressed pants always creasing at right angles perpendicular to the floor, and my most favorite part, the sweet little galoshes, rain or shine, just in case. My Byelinkov, never taken by surprise. Except by me.

BYELINKOV: You speak about me as if I were your pet.

VARINKA: You are my pet! My little school mouse.

BYELINKOV: A mouse?

VARINKA: My sweetest dancing bear with galoshes, my little stale babka.

BYELINKOV: A stale babka?

VARINKA: I am not Pushkin.

BYELINKOV (*Laughs*): That depends what you think of Pushkin.

VARINKA: You're smiling. I knew I could make you smile today.

BYELINKOV: I am a responsible man. Every day I have for breakfast black bread, fruit, hot tea, and every day I smile three times. I am halfway into my translation of the *Aeneid* from classical Greek hexameter into Russian alexandrines. In twenty years I have never been late to school. I am a responsible man, but no dancing bear.

VARINKA: Dance with me.

BYELINKOV: Now? It is nearly four weeks before the wedding!

VARINKA: It's a beautiful afternoon. We are in your garden. The roses are in full bloom.

BYELINKOV: The roses have beetles.

VARINKA: Dance with me!

BYELINKOV: You are a demanding woman.

VARINKA: You chose me. And right. And left. And turn. And right. And left.

BYELINKOV: And turn. Give me your hand. You dance like a school mouse. It's a beautiful afternoon! We are in my garden. The roses are in full bloom! And turn. And turn. (*Twirls* VARINKA *around*)

VARINKA: I am the luckiest woman!

   (BYELINKOV *stops dancing*)

Why are you stopping?

BYELINKOV: To place a lilac in your hair. Every year on this day I will place a lilac in your hair.

VARINKA: Will you remember?

BYELINKOV: I will write it down. (*Takes a notebook from his pocket*) Dear Byelinkov, don't forget the day a young lady, your bride, entered your garden, your peace, and danced on the roses. On that day every year you are to place a lilac in her hair.

VARINKA: I love you.

BYELINKOV: It is convenient we met.

VARINKA: I love you.

BYELINKOV: You are a girl.

VARINKA: I am thirty.

BYELINKOV: But you think like a girl. That is an attractive attribute.

VARINKA: Do you love me?

BYELINKOV: We've never spoken about housekeeping.

VARINKA: I am an excellent housekeeper. I kept house for my family on the farm in Gadyatchsky. I can make a beetroot soup with tomatoes and aubergines which is so nice. Awfully awfully nice.

BYELINKOV: You are fond of expletives.

VARINKA: My beet soup, sir, is excellent!

BYELINKOV: Please don't be cross. I too am an excellent housekeeper. I have a place for everything in the house. A shelf for each pot, a cubby for every spoon, a folder for favorite recipes. I have cooked for myself for twenty years. Though my beet soup is not outstanding, it is sufficient.

VARINKA: I'm sure it's very good.

BYELINKOV: No. It is awfully, awfully not. What I am outstanding in, however, what gives me greatest pleasure, is preserving those things which are left over. I wrap each tomato slice I haven't used in a wet cloth and place it in the coolest corner of the house. I have had my shoes for seven years because I wrap them in the galoshes you are so fond of. And every night before I go to sleep I wrap my bed in quilts and curtains so I never catch a draft.

VARINKA: You sleep with curtains on your bed?

BYELINKOV: I like to keep warm.

VARINKA: I will make you a new quilt.

BYELINKOV: No. No new quilt. That would be hazardous.

VARINKA: It is hazardous to sleep under curtains.

BYELINKOV: Varinka, I don't like change very much. If one works out the arithmetic the final fraction of improvement is at best less than an eighth of value over the total damage caused by disruption. I never thought of marrying till I saw your eyes dancing among the familiar faces at the headmaster's tea. I assumed I would grow old preserved like those which are left over, wrapped suitably in my case of curtains and quilts.

VARINKA: Byelinkov, I want us to have dinners with friends and summer country visits. I want people to say, "Have you spent time with Varinka and Byelinkov? He is so happy now that they are married. She is just what he needed."

BYELINKOV: You have already brought me some happiness. But I never was a sad man. Don't ever think I thought I was a sad man.

VARINKA: My sweetest darling, you can be whatever you want! If you are sad, they'll say she talks all the time, and he is soft-spoken and kind.

BYELINKOV: And if I am difficult?

VARINKA: Oh, they'll say he is difficult because he is highly intelligent. All great men are difficult. Look at Lermontov, Tchaikovsky, Peter the Great.

BYELINKOV: Ivan the Terrible.

VARINKA: Yes, him too.

BYELINKOV: Why are you marrying me? I am none of these things.

VARINKA: To me you are.

BYELINKOV: You have imagined this. You have constructed an elaborate romance for yourself. Perhaps you are the great one. You are the one with the great imagination.

VARINKA: Byelinkov, I am a pretty girl of thirty. You're right, I am not a woman. I have not made myself into a woman because I do not deserve that honor. Until I came to this town to visit my brother I lived on my family's farm. As the years passed I became younger and younger in fear that I would never marry. And it wasn't that I wasn't pretty enough or sweet enough, it was just that no man ever looked at me and saw a wife. I was not the woman who would be there when he came home. Until I met you I thought I would lie all my life and say I never married because I never met a man I loved. I will love you, Byelinkov. And I will help you to love me. We deserve the life everyone else has. We deserve not to be different.

BYELINKOV: Yes. We are the same as everyone else.

VARINKA: Tell me you love me.

BYELINKOV: I love you.

VARINKA (*Takes his hands*):   We will be very happy. I am very strong. (*Pauses*) It is time for tea.

BYELINKOV: It is too early for tea. Tea is at half past the hour.

VARINKA: Do you have heavy cream? It will be awfully nice with apricots.

BYELINKOV: Heavy cream is too rich for teatime.

VARINKA: But today is special. Today you placed a lilac in my hair. Write in your note pad. Every year we will celebrate with apricots and heavy cream. I will go to my brother's house and get some.

BYELINKOV: But your brother's house is a mile from here.

VARINKA: Today it is much shorter. Today my brother gave me his bicycle to ride. I will be back very soon.

BYELINKOV: You rode to my house by bicycle! Did anyone see you?

VARINKA: Of course. I had such fun. I told you I saw the grocery store lady with the son-in-law who is doing very well thank you in Moscow, and the headmaster's wife.

BYELINKOV: You saw the headmaster's wife!

VARINKA: She smiled at me.

BYELINKOV: Did she laugh or smile?

VARINKA: She laughed a little. She said, "My dear, you are very progressive to ride a bicycle." She said you and your fiancé Byelinkov must ride together sometime. I wonder if he'll take off his galoshes when he rides a bicycle.

BYELINKOV: She said that?

VARINKA: She adores you. We had a good giggle.

BYELINKOV: A woman can be arrested for riding a bicycle. That is not progressive, it is a premeditated revolutionary act. Your brother must be awfully, awfully careful on behalf of your behavior. He has been careless—oh so careless—in giving you the bicycle.

VARINKA: Dearest Byelinkov, you are wrapping yourself under curtains and quilts! I made friends on the bicycle.

BYELINKOV: You saw more than the headmaster's wife and the idiot grocery woman.

VARINKA: She is not an idiot.

BYELINKOV: She is a potato-vending, sausage-armed fool!

VARINKA: Shhhh! My school mouse. Shhh!

BYELINKOV: What other friends did you make on this bicycle?

VARINKA: I saw students from my brother's classes. They waved and shouted, "Anthropos in love! Anthropos in love!!"

BYELINKOV: Where is that bicycle?

VARINKA: I left it outside the gate. Where are you going?

BYELINKOV (*Muttering as he exits*):   Anthropos in love, anthropos in love.

VARINKA: They were cheering me on. Careful, you'll trample the roses.

BYELINKOV (*Returning with the bicycle*):   Anthropos is the Greek singular for man. Anthropos in love translates as the Greek and Latin master in love. Of course they cheered you. Their instructor, who teaches them the discipline and contained beauty of the classics, is in love with a sprite on a bicycle. It is a good giggle, isn't it? A very good giggle! I am returning this bicycle to your brother.

VARINKA: But it is teatime.

BYELINKOV: Today we will not have tea.

VARINKA: But you will have to walk back a mile.

BYELINKOV: I have my galoshes on. (*Gets on the bicycle*) Varinka, we deserve not to be different. (*Begins to pedal. The bicycle doesn't move*)

VARINKA: Put the kickstand up.

BYELINKOV: I beg your pardon.

VARINKA (*Giggling*):   Byelinkov, to make the bicycle move, you must put the kickstand up.

   (BYELINKOV *puts it up and awkwardly falls off the bicycle as it moves*)

(*Laughing*) Ha ha ha. My little school mouse. You look so funny! You are the sweetest dearest man in the world. Ha ha ha!

    (*Pause*)

BYELINKOV: Please help me up. I'm afraid my galosh is caught.

VARINKA (*Trying not to laugh*):   Your galosh is caught! (*Explodes in laughter again*) Oh, you are so funny! I do love you so. (*Helps* BYELINKOV *up*) You were right, my pet, as always. We don't need heavy cream for tea. The fraction of improvement isn't worth the damage caused by the disruption.

BYELINKOV: Varinka, it is still too early for tea. I must complete two stanzas of my translation before late afternoon. That is my regular schedule.

VARINKA: Then I will watch while you work.

BYELINKOV: No. You had a good giggle. That is enough.

VARINKA: Then while you work I will work too. I will make lists of guests for our wedding.

BYELINKOV: I can concentrate only when I am alone in my house. Please take your bicycle home to your brother.

VARINKA: But I don't want to leave you. You look so sad.

BYELINKOV: I never was a sad man. Don't ever think I was a sad man.

VARINKA: Byelinkov, it's a beautiful day, we are in your garden. The roses are in bloom.

BYELINKOV: Allow me to help you on to your bicycle. (*Takes* VARINKA'*s hand as she gets on the bike*)

VARINKA: You are such a gentleman. We will be very happy.

BYELINKOV: You are very strong. Good day, Varinka.

(VARINKA *pedals off.* BYELINKOV, *alone in the garden, takes out his pad and rips up the note about the lilac, strews it over the garden, then carefully picks up each piece of paper and places them all in a small envelope as lights fade to black*)

Vint

by

DAVID MAMET

CHARACTERS

PORTER

COMMISSIONER PERSOLIN

ZVISDULIN

KULAKEVITCH

NEDKUDOV

PSIULIN

A PORTER *and* COMMISSIONER PERSOLIN, *walking down the corridors of power, late at night.*

PORTER: You wish the coach to wait, your Excellency?

PERSOLIN: I've told him to. I just need the one file.

PORTER: I may say so, sir. It must be important, to drag you in so late.

PERSOLIN: It is, yes. It's for the Quarterly Report.

PORTER: Oh, yes, sir. Tomorrow's the day.

PERSOLIN: What's that I hear? (*Pauses*)

PORTER: Clerks, sir.

PERSOLIN: Clerks. (*Pauses*)

PORTER: Your clerks.

PERSOLIN: They're still here?

PORTER: Yessir.

PERSOLIN: They stayed to work on the report. God bless *them*. What is a man without his staff?

PORTER: As you say, Commissioner Persolin.

PERSOLIN: I think a commendation is in order here. (*Hands a slip of paper to* PORTER) Fetch me this file. (PORTER *goes off.* PERSOLIN *goes up to a door behind which we hear the clerks muttering. Speaks to himself*) My bully, bully boys . . .

ZVISDULIN (*Behind the door*):   My bid. An Interoffice Clerk.

KULAKEVITCH: Two Treasury.

PERSOLIN (*To himself*):   Two Treasury what?

NEDKUDOV: No, may we stop a moment, please?

ZVISDULIN: Finish the bidding. Eh?

PERSOLIN (*To himself*):   The bidding?

NEDKUDOV: Finish it *nothing*. Not at all. My partner leads an Interoffice Clerk, and then two *Treasury* . . . ?

KULAKEVITCH: It was my bid.

PERSOLIN (*To himself*):   What's going on here?

NEDKUDOV: All that I . . .

PSIULIN: It's his *bid*. Let it stand. When it's *your* bid, then *you* bid.

NEDKUDOV: All right . . . all right . . .

    (*Pause*)

PSIULIN: It's your bid.

NEDKUDOV: All right . . . two Treasury, and I raise . . . Vrazhansky.

KULAKEVITCH: Fine. Vrazhansky.

NEDKUDOV: Your bid . . . ?

PSIULIN: Madame Persolin.

(PERSOLIN *bursts in*)

PERSOLIN: What's going on here? (*Pauses*) I said, what's going on here?

KULAKEVITCH: Sir . . .

PERSOLIN: Yes. Sir. What? Come on. . . . Surprised to find you here, thought you were for once doing the work you're *paid* to, what do I . . . bandying the name of my wife. (*Pauses*) Now.

(*Pause*)

NEDKUDOV: Commissioner Persolin.

PERSOLIN: Now: What does this mean?

(*Pause*)

ZVISDULIN: We . . .

PERSOLIN: Yes. What what what? Up all night . . . finish the report—I come in. I . . . *What are you doing?*

KULAKEVITCH: We were playing cards.

(*Pause*)

PERSOLIN: Playing cards. And bandying the name of my wife.

ZVISDULIN: Yes. As you see . . . playing cards and . . .

PERSOLIN: Ignorant as I am it seems to me those are not cards but Identity Dossiers.

(*Pause*)

NEDKUDOV: Yes, sir, that's what they are.

PERSOLIN: That's what they are.

NEDKUDOV: Yes. Sir.

PERSOLIN: So what is it I'm privy to? In this perversion? In this
. . . this unauthorized use of . . . Treason? I would have
thought you lacked the initiative. But. No. Unauthorized files,
you . . .

KULAKEVITCH: We assure you, sir. We. We were only playing
vint.

PERSOLIN: Playing vint.

KULAKEVITCH: Yessir.

(*Pause*)

PERSOLIN: With Identity Dossiers.

KULAKEVITCH: Yes, sir.

PERSOLIN: And how *is* that? Well. Let me *profit* from it, *please*.

(*Pause*)

NEDKUDOV (*To* KULAKEVITCH):   *You* go.

(*Pause*)

KULAKEVITCH: Um. Each name, you see, your Excellency . . .

PERSOLIN: Yes . . .

KULAKEVITCH: Each name is like a card. Just like a regular deck.
Four suits. Fifty-two cards. Men of the Treasury are hearts,
the Provincial Administrators clubs, the State Bank spades,
the Ministry of Education . . . and so on, you see . . . State
Councilors are aces, Assistant State Councilors . . .

NEDKUDOV: It's very easy, sir . . . and down the line. Collegiate
Councilors jacks, their wives are queens . . .

PERSOLIN: . . . wives of the Collegiate Councilors . . .

KULAKEVITCH: . . . are queens . . . Court Councilors are tens,
and so on. I . . . here's *my* card: Stepan Kulakevitch: three.

PERSOLIN: You're a three.

KULAKEVITCH: Three of, yessir, the three of clubs. And Zvisdulin, here, he's a—

PERSOLIN: What am I?

(*Pause*)

ZVISDULIN: Ace of clubs.

(*Pause*)

PERSOLIN: I'm the ace of clubs.

KULAKEVITCH: Yessir.

PERSOLIN: And my wife?

KULAKEVITCH: Is the queen of clubs.

PERSOLIN: You said the queen was the spouse of the jack.

ZVISDULIN: As the jack in Provincial has no wife . . .

PERSOLIN: Ah.

KULAKEVITCH (*Confidentially*): It's Mosischev . . .

PERSOLIN: Yes, I know.

ZVISDULIN: . . . and neither the king, we took the liberty . . .

KULAKEVITCH: . . . and meant no disre—

PERSOLIN: Yes, yes, yes, and so my wife's the queen of clubs.

(*Pause*)

NEDKUDOV: Yessir.

PERSOLIN: And as I came in she'd just—

PSIULIN: I'd had the honor to *bid* her.

NEDKUDOV: As you came in she'd just taken a trick over two Treasury half-councilors.

PERSOLIN: She did.

NEDKUDOV: Yes.

PERSOLIN: And who were they?

KULAKEVITCH (*Checks*):   Ostopchin and Brot.

(*Pause*)

PERSOLIN: And she took that trick.

KULAKEVITCH: Yes.

NEDKUDOV: You see, he led the Interoffice Clerk. Why? *Why*, I said . . .

KULAKEVITCH: I countered with the Treasury.

PERSOLIN: Why make the diamonds vulnerable?

NEDKUDOV: That's what *I* said. That's what *I* said!

PERSOLIN: And so you've got to come back with my wife.

NEDKUDOV: Wasted a perfectly good queen. With all resp—

PERSOLIN: No, you're quite right. Wasted. Yes. Who taught you to play? He leads who? The Interoffice . . . ?

ZVISDULIN: Brulin and Baschenko.

PERSOLIN: He leads Brulin. Brulin *and* Baschenko?

ZVISDULIN: Yes.

PERSOLIN: *Why?*

ZVISDULIN: To force—

PERSOLIN: You know . . . you're laying the whole Ministry open to—

NEDKUDOV: That's what *I* said.

PERSOLIN: Look—look—can I get in?

KULAKEVITCH: Sir, we'd be honored to—

NEDKUDOV: Give him the cards.

ZVISDULIN: Deal him in.

(PERSOLIN *is dealt in*)

PERSOLIN: All right. Now: let's go back to *you*.

PSIULIN: I bid your wife.

PERSOLIN: My bid?

PSIULIN: Yes.

PERSOLIN: All right. Grand Court Councilor, I give you: Ivan Dimich Grelandsky.

(*Pause*)

NEDKUDOV: Brilliant.

PERSOLIN: Well, you *see* . . . ?

NEDKUDOV: Brilliant.

PERSOLIN: If he comes out with Education . . .

KULAKEVITCH: Yes . . .

PERSOLIN: What do I have? Look: let's play this hand open. I have *Grelandsky* . . . Paschin . . .

NEDKUDOV: Yes.

(*The* PORTER *sticks his head in*)

PORTER: Excellency, I have the file.

PERSOLIN (*Brushing him off*): Just . . . just . . . just . . .

NEDKUDOV: Finish the hand: the man bid Grelandsky.

KULAKEVITCH: All right. Grelandsky, and . . . has Potkin fallen?

PSIULIN: No, we're void in Education.

PORTER: Excellency . . . ?

PERSOLIN (*Sternly*):   Will you *please* . . . ?

KULAKEVITCH: All right. Grelandsky and . . . um . . . um . . .

NEDKUDOV: No prompting.

KULAKEVITCH: And . . . um . . .

PERSOLIN: Just bid, will you?

KULAKEVITCH: All right, I . . .

PERSOLIN: What are you, working by the *hour*? Come *on*. Come on!

Drowning

by

MARIA IRENE FORNES

CHARACTERS

PEA

ROE

STEPHEN

S C E N E   I

A café, probably in Europe. PEA and ROE sit at a table. PEA to the right, ROE to the left. It is late afternoon. There is a lot of olive green in the air and the trimmings are olive green enamel. PEA's and ROE's heads are large and shapeless, like potatoes. Their skin is dark. Their flesh is shiny and oily. Their eyes are reddish and watery. They have warts on their faces and necks. Their bodies are also like potatoes. PEA wears an olive hat, a beige jacket, and greenish-brown pants. ROE wears a brown hat and a brown suit. When they breathe their bodies sweat. Their skin and general shape resemble those of seals or sea lions. There is a folded newspaper on the table. PEA looks at it.

PEA: My God, what is it?

ROE: It's a newspaper.

PEA: It is beautiful. (ROE *nods*) May I touch it? (ROE *nods*. PEA *touches the paper. A tear rolls down his face*) This must be made by a person.

ROE: Yes, many of them. They put out a new one each day.

(PEA *lifts the corner of the first page. He gasps. He puts the palm of his hand on the paper tenderly. He takes his hand off and looks at it again*)

PEA (*Pointing*):   Is this not a woman?

ROE: Yes.

PEA (*Pointing*):   And what is this?

(ROE *looks*)

ROE: A snowdrift. (PEA *looks at* ROE) It is snow that has been blown by the wind. (*Looks at the caption*) It's seven feet high.

PEA: It is very high.

ROE: Yes.

PEA: What is snow?

ROE: Snow is rain that freezes as it falls to the ground. It freezes with the cold. It becomes white and it is not liquid. It is more like powder. (*Pointing*) You see here? They have made a snow-man.

PEA: A man?

ROE: Not a real man. They have packed the snow and shaped it so it resembles a man.

PEA: How awkward.

ROE: Why is it awkward?

PEA: Oh, isn't it?

ROE: Well no, I think it's very well made.

PEA: Oh yes! It's very well made.

ROE: I thought you found it awkward.

PEA: Maybe I don't know what awkward means.

ROE: Oh, awkward means clumsy, not graceful.

PEA: Oh, I meant to say strikingly wonderful.

ROE: Oh, awkward doesn't mean that.

PEA: Oh, well. I must apologize then. The man is very well made.

ROE: Oh, you don't need to apologize. He doesn't mind your saying he's awkward.

PEA: He is very nice then. He must be a very nice man.

ROE: He's not a man.

PEA: I thought you said he was.

ROE: He is a snowman. That is, he is an imitation of a man. It is snow that has been packed to look like a man.

PEA: What am I made of?

ROE: You're made of flesh. Human flesh.

PEA: And you?

ROE: Human flesh.

PEA (*Pointing to the paper*):   And her?

ROE: She's made of human flesh.

PEA (*Pointing*):   I look more like him than like her.

ROE (*Looks closely at the picture*):   Maybe. (*Short pause*) But he, when it gets warmer, will melt. She will not. And you will not.

PEA: Could I meet her?

ROE: You want to meet her?

PEA: Yes.

ROE (*Reads the caption*): Her name is Jane Spivak.

PEA: She's beautiful. I would like to look at her. In the flesh.

ROE: I don't know if I could introduce you to her. I don't know where she lives. But I know other girls I could introduce you to.

PEA: I don't think I want to meet anyone else. Other girls may be beautiful, but she looks so very lovely. I like looking at her. (*Touching the paper*) Even here on this paper. (*Pauses*) We should be leaving now, Roe, before it gets cold.

ROE: We should wait for Stephen. He said he would meet us here.

PEA: He did?

ROE: Yes.

PEA: At what time did he say he will come?

ROE: At six.

(STEPHEN *enters*)

Here he is. (*Reaches for his cane*) We can leave now.

PEA: He may want to stay awhile and warm up.

ROE: Oh, yes, he may.

(STEPHEN *looks like* PEA *and* ROE. *He wears a brown hat, a small checkered jacket, and brown pants. He waddles toward the table. The lights fade*)

S C E N E   2

A few minutes later. PEA's head leans on the table. He sleeps. ROE sits on the left. STEPHEN stands upstage of the table.

STEPHEN (*Referring to* PEA):   He is very kind and he could not do harm to anyone.

ROE: Yes. And I don't want any harm to come to him either because he's good.

(*The lights fade*)

S C E N E   3

A month later. PEA sits in the same seat. ROE stands to his left. PEA's necktie is pulled loose. His shirt collar is open and his hat is pushed back as someone who has not slept well. He is somewhat frenetic.

PEA: She is a mystery to me. I look at her as one looks at an animal, loving those eyes, the look in them, the breath as it goes into her shirt, her lips as they close and then part, her mind, the way her body moves. I love her. She is close to my heart the way only an animal can be. And as unfathomable. Looking into her eyes is so quiet—like sleep, like a bed. And she, she is wild like a tiger. She smells like a lion, and she claws like a lion, and yet, in her eyes, she is quiet like a fish.

ROE: That is beautiful, Pea, the way you talk about her.

PEA (*Short of air and making a sound like snoring*):   I am not a person. I am a bat. Look at my skin, see? It is too smooth and too dark. Touch it. This is not like human skin. Look at my nails.

Press them. (ROE *presses* PEA's *fingers*) See how they turn white?
That's not human. (*Stands and turns his buttocks in* ROE's *direction*)
Look at that. My anus is violet. Put your finger on it. It is
rough. (*Sits*) When I met her I asked her if it felt as good to
touch her as it felt to look at her. She said, "Try it." (*Moves his
head up and from side to side rapturously*) Do you know what it is
to need someone? The feeling is much deeper than words can
ever say. Do you know what despair is? Anguish? What is it
that makes someone a link between you and your own life? I
hold her close to me and she pushes me away. She finds me
repulsive. She pushed me away and she said, "You rub against
me like a piece of meat. You are a piece of meat. That's what
you are. Like meat at the meat market. You have no brains or
a soul. You are just a piece of meat. Don't rub against me anymore."

ROE (*Putting his hand on* PEA's *forehead*):   Let me touch you. You
are cold. What a terrible thing to see a young man like you
destroyed like this. Suffering like this.

PEA (*Gets the folded newspaper from inside his jacket*):   I thought if I
kept her picture next to me I'd find relief. But I don't find
relief. There is no relief in this. (*Puts his head on the table*) Is this
why we have come to life? To love like this? And hurt like this?

> (*A moment passes.* ROE *puts his hand on* PEA's *back.* STEPHEN
> *enters and waddles to the table. He looks at* ROE)

ROE: He's drowning. He hurts too much.

> (*Lights fade to black*)

A Dopey Fairy Tale

by

MICHAEL WELLER

CHARACTERS

SMILE

FATHER BAKER

MOTHER BAKER

CLARENCE

CHATTER (the dog)

MAYOR

MAGISTRATE

MINISTER

FEMALE FROG

MALE FROG

SAD PRINCESS GLADYS

This should all be played real dopey.

> *Enter* SMILE, *the narrator, in a swallowtail coat and top hat, and an enormous fixed smile that never leaves his face.*

SMILE: Once upon a very long time ago, in a far distant fairy-tale kingdom in the tiny village of, oh, say, Placeville, there lived a family of jolly bakers.

> (*Lights up on family group:* FATHER, MOTHER, CLARENCE, *and* CHATTER, *a dog*)

SMILE: There was the jolly father, Mr. Baker . . .

FATHER: Pie, bread, cookies, cake,
These are the things I like to bake.

SMILE: His jolly, good-hearted, but somewhat impractical wife, Mrs. Baker . . .

MOTHER: The Smiths ordered two loaves of pumpernickel bread, but I threw in a dozen chocolate chip cookies for free because they love them so much and even though we may end up losing money, still, just think how happy the Smiths will be.

FATHER: You're so impractical, dear.

MOTHER: But I'm very good-hearted.

SMILE: Then there was Chatter the dog, who could do something most dogs can't.

CHATTER (*Digging*):   I could have sworn I buried that bone right here in the front yard . . . !

SMILE: He could talk!

CHATTER: Or was it the backyard? Or under the willow by the river?

SMILE: But he had a terrible terrible memory.

CHATTER (*To* SMILE):   I can talk, can't I? Give a dog a break.

SMILE: And last, but most important of all, was their son Clarence, who until recently had been a very ordinary little boy, until he discovered that he had a very extraordinary talent.

CLARENCE (*Imitating* SMILE):   "Once upon a very long time ago, in the tiny village of, oh, say, Placeville . . ."

SMILE: He could imitate anyone he met . . . perfectly.

CLARENCE: "Perfectly."

SMILE: Isn't that adorable?

FATHER: You be careful who you make fun of, boy. Not everyone likes to see themselves in a comical light.

CLARENCE: I don't mean any harm, Father, sir. I just enjoy seeing people laugh. . . .

SMILE: Every year, the ruler of the kingdom, the orphaned regent Sad Princess Gladys, would wander from the royal palace for one entire month.

(PRINCESS GLADYS *crosses stage singing the first phrase of* "Stormy Weather")

Where she went no one knew, but when she returned, she held a royal feast and each village in the kingdom sent to her table the one dish they made best. For one's village to send one's dish was a great, great honor.

FATHER: Mother, Clarence, Chatter, guess who's coming to pay us a visit tomorrow? The Mayor, the Minister, and the Magistrate.

MOTHER: The Three Big M's of Placeville? But, dear, they would only visit us at this time of year if . . .

FATHER: That's right! They have agreed to sample our pastries and consider them for the official entry of Placeville at the royal feast of Sad Princess Gladys. If chosen, we'll be summoned to the palace in a royal coach, the Princess will allow us to grovel at her feet, word will spread, our pastry will become famous throughout the land, we'll open a chain of stores . . . McBaker's! Invest in real estate. Diversify. We'll be rich, rich, rich!

CHATTER: I'm so excited I could bark, if I remembered how!

(FAMILY *sets up table of pastries*)

SMILE: So all that night the Bakers baked in preparation for their important visitors, and while the town slept peacefully, the dark air filled with savory odors from the Bakers' chimney: jam tarts and quince tarts and rhubarb pie and veal pie and chocolate chip cookies and oatmeal raisin cookies and blueberry muffins and egg bread and sesame rolls and strawberry flans and cinnamon doughnuts and honey popovers and cannoli. No, wait, not cannoli. I'm getting carried away. I just happen to love cannoli. Have you ever tasted it with espresso cof— (*Stops*) Never mind. The next morning, when all was ready, Father Baker called his family together.

FATHER: Now, Clarence, remember, we must do everything in

our power to please the Three Big M's of Placeville, so be polite at all times, speak only when spoken to, and, above all, none of your infernal imitations. The punch, Mother . . . explain.

MOTHER: There are two bowls of punch. The one at this end of the table has in it a little something to make our honored guests feel pleasant and look kindly upon our baked goods. The one at this end is plain old punch. Children and dogs drink from this one. The rest of us from the other.

CLARENCE: Yes, Mother.

MOTHER: Chatter?

CHATTER: Under the shed! That's where I buried it. What? Oh, yes, I understand.

SMILE: And with that, the guests arrived.

(*Enter* MAYOR, MINISTER, *and* MAGISTRATE, *all very self-important*)

FATHER: Mr. Mayor, Mr. Minister, Mr. Magistrate, what an honor to have you with us today. Please, help yourselves.

MAYOR (*With flourishes*): And what a delectable array of the baker's art you have endeavored to present before us on this hallowed day of sampling and decision. The smell alone arouses within my person elements of compliment which I would hasten to utter if time and circumstances were of a more flexible aspect, but that being not the case, let us eschew becoming lost in the byways of preamble, and to the tasting!

MOTHER: Chatter, some punch for the guests.

(CHATTER *obeys, putting punch in cups and passing them out*)

FATHER: And how do you enjoy the pineapple upside-down cake, Mr. Minister?

MINISTER: F-f-f-f-first rate, I m-m-m-must say.

MOTHER: Mr. Magistrate, those are the chocolate éclairs, one of our specialties.

MAGISTRATE: Are they not topped with chocolate? This is visible. Have they not the oblong shape of éclairs? This is patent. So, altogether, are they not chocolate éclairs? Of this I'm aware.

CHATTER (*With two cups*):   This one's for you, Clarence, and this one's for the Mayor. No, wait. This one . . . right paw, left paw. Which paw do you eat your soup with? Oh! I remember now. *This* one's yours.

CLARENCE (*Drinking*):   Aren't they silly, Chatter. I bet if they could see themselves, they'd howl with laughter.

CHATTER: Remember what your father said, Clarence.

CLARENCE: I know, I know.

CHATTER: What *did* he say? There was something you shouldn't do. Or was it *should*?

MAYOR: Mr. and Mrs. Baker, may I just say that even having concluded a mere fraction of the available sampling here before us, I find myself vigorously propelled towards a favorable reception vis-à-vis the fruits of your artistry, if I may put it that way.

MAGISTRATE: Is the flavor not superior? This has been experienced. Might our town take pride in such an entry? This is possible.

MINISTER: D-d-d-d-d-d-d-d-d-d-d-dee-li-li-li-li-li-licious.

FATHER: Well, Mother, what do you say to that?

MOTHER (*After a pause*):   Have seconds!

(ALL *laugh politely*)

FATHER: Clarence, would you like to thank our guests?

CLARENCE (*Looking woozy*): Th-th-th-th-thank you o-o-o-one and all.

MINISTER (*Pleased*): It's n-n-n-nothing, my b-b-b-. What did he just s-s-s-s-say?

MOTHER: Clarence!

CHATTER (*To himself*): Left paw, right paw. Uh-oh.

MAGISTRATE: Was your son not mocking the Minister? This is suggested.

CLARENCE: And is the suggestion not amusing? It is. Are we not on the verge of laughter? We should be.

FATHER: Not another word, Clarence. Go directly to your room.

MAYOR: Am I receiving the impression that your son's behavioral peculiarity contains within it elements of imitation which could be taken to reflect upon certain members of the company present in the area of this room today?

CLARENCE: The behavioral aspects in question contain within their limits only a desire to illustrate to the collected population within the purviews of the area under our roof a certain humorous impression . . .

MINISTER: He's making f-f-f-f-fun of us.

CLARENCE: You're making f-f-f-fun of yourself.

MAGISTRATE: Is my temper not rising at this display? This is tangible. Am I not about to explode with anger? This is imminent.

CLARENCE: Do you not always answer your own questions? This we've observed.

FATHER: To your room!

CLARENCE: Is anyone interested in what you have to say? This is doubtful.

MAYOR: How dare you! Take that! (*Hits* CLARENCE) And that. (*Hits him again*) And that and that and that.

(THE THREE BIG M'*s pounce on* CLARENCE *and beat him*)

MOTHER: Stop, you bullies, he's only a little boy!

FATHER: Perhaps now he'll know better than to disobey his father!

MOTHER: Chatter, do something to frighten them off. Bark. Growl. Be menacing.

CHATTER (*Pronouncing the words*): Arf. Arf. Grrr. Grrr. Bark. Rolf. Woof-woof. Something's lacking.

(*The beating stops*)

MAYOR: Needless to articulate, no elements of the baker's trade will represent this village at the royal feast, this year or ever!

MINISTER: P-p-p-p-astries be damned.

MAGISTRATE: Are we not leaving in a huff? We are!

(THE THREE BIG M'*s exit in a huff*)

MOTHER: Oh, Clarence, darling, are you all right?

CLARENCE: Why did they do that, Mother? I thought they'd find it funny.

FATHER: They're laughing, all right. And guess who's the joke? No meeting with Sad Princess Gladys. No McBaker's. All our dreams in ruins. Tomorrow you will come with me and apologize to the Three Big Ms of Placeville. We will humble ourselves before them and beg to have our pastry reconsidered!

CLARENCE: How can I apologize when I did nothing wrong?

FATHER: Are you contradicting me, young man?

MOTHER: Don't be so hard on him, dear. He only meant to amuse.

FATHER: I'm locking you in your room until you agree to come with me and apologize. No back talk. Go to your room.

SMILE: And so, that night, Clarence was locked up alone in his room, while Chatter sat outside the door listening to his beloved friend's sighs. Oh, dear, this part's so sad, I can barely bring myself to watch.

(CHATTER *and* CLARENCE *on opposite sides of make-believe door*)

CHATTER: How ya doin', Clar?

CLARENCE: Sigh.

CHATTER: Oh, boy. My screw-up. There I was, one of each punch in separate cups, and then I remembered . . . it's under the bench in the town square, that's where I buried my bone. And everything else went clean out of my head. (*Pauses*) Clar, talk to me. (*Pauses*) God, when you did the Mayor I was so near laughing out loud I nearly had to run and find a tree to pee on. Do him again, I really get a kick out of that one. Clar?

CLARENCE (*After a pause, trying*):   I . . . I can't.

CHATTER: Why not?

CLARENCE: Nothing comes out.

CHATTER: The Magistrate, he's easy, I can almost handle that one myself.

CLARENCE (*After a pause*):   It's no use, Chatter. I try and try, but all I remember is their angry faces and how they beat me, and nothing comes out.

CHATTER: Bad attitude, Clar.

CLARENCE: Well, what else am I to think?

CHATTER: Try this on for size. "Where there's life, there's hope." And how about "Every cloud has a silver lining." (*Pauses*) Darn, there's another one . . . it's right on the tip of my tongue. "Go for it," that's the one.

CLARENCE: Go for what?

CHATTER: Your talent. We'll venture forth to search for where it went, and we'll have some adventures, and then we'll find it and we can all live happily ever after.

CLARENCE: You're right, Chatter! Why didn't I think of that? But first I have to escape from my room.

CHATTER: Leave that part to me.

SMILE: And so Chatter, using skills he'd acquired here and there, picked the lock on Clarence's bedroom door, and that night two figures could be seen slipping across the shadows of the village square, out past the fields of the surrounding farms, across the river and into the dark dark forest beyond. After what seemed like hours, it dawned on them that they were lost.

CLARENCE: Chatter, where are we?

CHATTER: Well, I'm over here and you're over there. After that it's anyone's guess.

SMILE: Now comes the scary bit. I love to be frightened. Like when someone sneaks up behind you and goes "Boo!" Isn't that great? Anyway, all around them, the frightened pair heard strange noises from the depths of the dark dark forest.

(*Strange animal noises*)

CLARENCE: Boy, Chatter, there's sure some spooky noises in the forest.

CHATTER: That's not the only spooky thing, Clar. Look up ahead!

CLARENCE: What is it?

CHATTER: Whatever it is, there's two of them. A pair of spooky things.

> (*Enter* TWO FROGS, *a* MALE—M.F.—*and a* FEMALE—F.F.— *hopping*)

BOTH FROGS: Ribbit-ribbit. Ribbit-ribbit.

CLARENCE: They sound like frogs.

CHATTER: They sound like *big* frogs.

CLARENCE: Try talking to them.

CHATTER: Clarence, frogs don't talk.

CLARENCE: Neither do dogs.

CHATTER: Good point, good point. Hey, you two. You two frogs! What's the deal here?

F.F.:   We are enchanted frogs.

CHATTER: Enchanted frogs, God, what an image.

F.F.:   You're here because you think you've lost your talent, Clarence. But it isn't true. All you have lost is the courage to use it. You must find your courage, and once you've found it, you must never again let it go, no matter how angry it may make people.

CLARENCE: But where shall I look?

F.F.:   We're coming to that, take it easy.

M.F.:   You start, dear.

F.F.:   Only one person in the kingdom can help you, Clarence, and that is the orphaned regent Sad Princess Gladys. Seek her out, discover what makes her sad, then find a way to bring a smile to her face, for it is written that he who makes the princess smile shall one day be king.

M.F.:   And being a king is a very big deal. If that doesn't restore your courage, forget it.

CLARENCE: But this is the month the princess disappears, to whence no one knows. How shall I ever find her?

F.F.:   You must undergo the following trial. Do exactly as we say and no harm shall come to you. But one mistake and, poof, you'll both be turned to Dacron.

M.F.:   Rock, darling. They'll be turned to rock.

F.F.:   Whatever. First, you must walk straight ahead in the direction we point, and for three days and three nights you may not stop, nor may you look to the right or to the left.

M.F.:   On the third day . . .

F.F.:   And no food. You can't eat anything.

M.F.:   That's right. Then, on day three, a great rain will fall, and before a single droplet can touch you, you must say the words "Gladys, where art thou and what makes thee so sad?" Whereupon you will become tiny enough to walk between the raindrops, and this is very important . . .

F.F.:   . . . because if you are wet when you reach the Mighty Oak of Oaks, you will be turned instantly into mohair.

M.F.:   Rock, dear.

F.F.:   You tell it your way, I'll tell it mine. Have you both understood?

CLARENCE: Are you getting all this, Chatter?

CHATTER: You lost me at the raindrops.

M.F.:   At the Mighty Oak of Oaks, you will find lying nearby a stick in the shape of a Y. This you must beat against the tree. The rain will stop instantly, a bolt of lightning will strike the oak and render it in twain . . .

CLARENCE: Is all this really necessary? It sounds awfully complicated.

F.F.:   You want to know if there's a shortcut, sonny? Of course there's a shortcut, there's always a shortcut.

CLARENCE: Perhaps you could tell us what it is.

M.F.:   If we had wanted to do that, we'd have told you in the first place. We're enchanted frogs. We call the shots.

F.F.:   You want to do it your way, go ahead, see what happens, but don't expect any help from us. And remember, one wrong move, hello mohair.

M.F.:   Ribbit-ribbit.

(BOTH FROGS *exit*)

CLARENCE: No, wait . . .

SMILE: As the enchanted frogs leapt away, Clarence realized with growing horror what a desperate situation they were in.

CLARENCE: Oh, Chatter, now what do we do? One wrong move and we'll be fabric.

CHATTER: Let me think. I've been in this situation before.

CLARENCE: You have?

CHATTER: Oh, you know, other fairy tales. The faithful companion, that sort of thing.

CLARENCE: You've been in other fairy tales?

CHATTER: Did you think I was a one-tale dog? The thing is, there was always a way out.

SMILE: Whereupon Chatter, barely knowing why, but overwhelmed with a certainty that he was very close to the bone, set to digging with a frenzy.

(CHATTER *digs with a fury*)

CHATTER: Oh, yes, that smell, that smell. A nice, juicy tibia. And with bits of meat still clinging to the ends, if memory serves. (*Finds something*) I've got something. This isn't a bone.

CLARENCE: It's a diamond, Chatter. It's the largest diamond I ever saw.

CHATTER: Just my luck. Go for a meal, end up with a rock.

CLARENCE: Listen, it's starting to hum.

CHATTER: Great. A humming diamond, just what I need. Next thing you know, it'll probably talk.

VOICE: Who are you two, and what brings you here?

CHATTER: What did I tell you!

CLARENCE: No, Chatter, look over there . . . !

SMILE: As they turned, they beheld the most beautiful creature they had ever seen. Her lips were like pearls. Rubies, sorry, rubies. Her skin was like pearls. Or alabaster. Also, she looked very sad.

PRINCESS: How did you know where to find the diamond from my missing father's crown?

CLARENCE: We are looking for the orphaned regent, Sad Princess Gladys.

PRINCESS: Look no more.

CHATTER: You don't understand, lady, we have important business with the woman.

PRINCESS: I am she who you seek.

CLARENCE: But you . . . you're . . . beautiful.

PRINCESS: I know. Beautiful . . . and sad.

CHATTER (*After a pause*):   Is that it? Have we done it?

CLARENCE: First we must learn why she's sad, then I must make her smile.

CHATTER: Why?

CLARENCE: To get back my courage.

CHATTER: Oh, right, right. You go ahead, I'll cover you from behind. Wait, that's a different fairy tale. Or was it a western?

CLARENCE: Princess Gladys . . .

CHATTER: Clar, was I in a western?

CLARENCE: Princess Gladys, I've been seeking you to ask a question. What makes you so sad? Will you answer?

PRINCESS: Since you discovered where I buried the largest diamond from my missing father's crown . . . yes. I will tell you what I've told no living creature before this day. I am in mourning for my life. No, that's wrong. I am a seagull. No, that's not it.

CHATTER: She's a real hoot, this one.

PRINCESS: I am forever sad because my mother and father, who others knew as the king and queen because that is what they were, disappeared when I was first born, spirited away by a witch, they say, and by a magic spell turned into creatures of another species. Each year I take a month off to look for them in the woods, petting all the animals I find, hoping thereby to recognize, by a touch or a gesture, some sign of my heritage. Each year I fail, alas, and then I return to the palace and hold a feast to help take my mind off it. Eating sometimes helps. It's a form of substitute behavior common among the well-to-do, and I'm no exception.

CLARENCE: If you were a mere baby when they disappeared, isn't it time to stop being sad?

PRINCESS: But I don't wish to stop. And even if I wished to, it would be wrong, terribly wrong. You see, it's good to be sad. I want everyone in my kingdom to be sad in every part of their body, just as I am. My skin is sad, my hands are sad, my hair is by . . . no, that's not it. My eyes are sad, my lips are sad, and I could cry until I melt into a warm puddle of salt tears.

(CLARENCE, *without realizing it, starts to imitate her*)

CLARENCE: And then my tears will mix with the soil and water all the land until trees grow sad and the grass grows sad and the rivers run sadly through the kingdom . . .

PRINCESS: Are you making fun of me, commoner?

CLARENCE: And even then I won't be satisfied until the clouds breathe in my tears from the forest and cause the rain to fall sad and the wind to blow sad and the entire world to weep and weep and weep.

PRINCESS: I am a princess. Keep it up and I'll make a lot of trouble for you.

CLARENCE: I'm your subject. Keep it up and you'll make a lot of trouble for me.

(CLARENCE *is now enjoying it*)

PRINCESS: One more word and I shall strike you with my royal open palm.

CLARENCE: But sadly, princess, do it sadly.

(PRINCESS *raises her hand to strike. Stops*)

PRINCESS: Is that really the way I look?

CHATTER: He's got you down to a tee, lady.

PRINCESS (*Smiles, then laughs*):   That's ridiculous. You mean I've been going around all these years looking like that? Why didn't someone tell me? (*Laughs*) I could die with shame if it wasn't so funny.

CHATTER: Hey, Clar, do you realize what you just did? You imitated her. And she's laughing!

CLARENCE: It just came out. She looked in my eyes, and I don't know . . . it gave me courage. Is that what love is?

(*Enter* FROGS)

F.F.:   Look, dear, she's laughing.

M.F.:   If she laughs, the spell is broken. We forgot to say that part.

(BOTH FROGS *stand up straight, now the* KING *and* QUEEN)

QUEEN: Darling!

KING: My dear daughter.

PRINCESS: Mother? Father? It's really you. And guess what, I'm in love. With him. What's your name?

CLARENCE: Clarence.

PRINCESS: Can I marry him, please, please, please?

QUEEN: Sure.

PRINCESS: Thanks.

KING: Welcome, Clarence, to the royal family, ribbit-rib . . . whoops.

SMILE: And with that, Clarence returned home a hero, and Placeville welcomed him with open arms.

>(*Enter* FATHER, MOTHER, MAYOR, MAGISTRATE, *and* MINISTER)

MOTHER: My son, the king!

FATHER: Good boy, good good boy.

MAYOR: We're pleased and anxious to suck up to certain elements of the newly returned royal personage.

MINISTER: His ass-ass-ass-ass-astonishing talent, in particul-l-l-l-lar.

MAGISTRATE: A question? An answer!

SMILE: So Mr. Baker got his franchise, Clarence regained his talent forever, and year after year the palace rang with laughter as he imitated everyone in sight. And at long long last, Chatter found his bone.

>(SMILE *removes bone from inside pocket, or produces it like magic.* CHATTER, *behind him, approaches the bone, but the moment before he clamps his jaw around it,* SMILE *remembers something and begins to speak, waving the bone oblivious of* CHATTER, *who stands right behind him, trying to grab it with his mouth*)

The moral?

ALL: The moral.

SMILE: If you have a talent, don't be frightened when it upsets people . . . because one day you'll marry a princess and no one will dare mess with you! Not very universal, is it? I'm terrible at ends. How about . . . let's see . . . pompous behavior deserves to be laughed at? Or . . . don't pooh-pooh large frogs in the forest, they may be royalty. Or this: Anton Chekhov was a great writer, but when you quote him out of context even his dialogue sounds laughable. Or . . .

CHATTER: Give a dog a break.

(SMILE *hands him the bone*)

SMILE: And they all lived happily ever after.

CLARENCE (*Like* SMILE):   Because I commanded it, and I was the king.

SMILE: The end.

(ALL *bow and exit*)

Eve of the Trial

by

SAMM-ART WILLIAMS

CHARACTERS

MA LOLA
: Owns a run-down rural rooming house just outside Baton Rouge, Louisiana.

LESTER SIMMONS
: The "hanging judge" in charge of the Circuit Court in Baton Rouge. Southern.

PEARL SIMMONS
: Lester's wife. Southern.

TATE
: A deputy sheriff from Baton Rouge, who is assigned to take Alex and his two wives to Baton Rouge to stand trial for bigamy.

ALEX BUSHKIN (ALEXIS BUSKENOV)
: Russian expatriate now stranded in the southern United States as a result of the Bolshevik Revolution, which saw his family give their property to the state. Alex believes that the Bolsheviks are going to assassinate him, so he marries two women and sets out for Utah, where he will live in disguise as a Mormon. Educated, Western manner, pompous. Very charming to the ladies.

LILLY
: One of Alex's wives. Lilly once worked in the Scarlet Garter, a whorehouse in Charleston, South Carolina. Southern.

KITTY
: One of Alex's wives. Kitty is a good friend of Lilly's and is also an ex-employee of the Scarlet Garter. Southern.

Time: August 1919
Place: Ma Lola's rooming house just outside Baton Rouge,
Louisiana
Set units: 1. Living room, sparsely furnished, with kerosene
lamps
2. Bare stage area
Note: The weather is hot, humid, and sticky. The mosquitoes
bite with a vengeance and one's clothing seldom dries from yes-
terday's sweat. Not to mention that the air seldom moves in this
part of Louisiana. Especially at . . . midnight.

> *It is midnight. Lights come up on the interior of* MA LOLA's
> *rooming house. The furnishings are spare and rustic. The house
> in general is a filthy mess. As the lights come up, we hear the
> sound of crickets and the hooting of an owl.* MA LOLA, PEARL,
> *and* LESTER *enter the living room.* LESTER *is tired and weary.*
> PEARL *is nursing stomach cramps from an advanced case of diar-
> rhea.* MA *lights a kerosene lamp, stage left. Suddenly* MA *shouts
> aloud and stomps on a water bug several times.*

MA: Ahhhh! Ahhhh! Little varmints! Damn little varmints!

LESTER: Jesus Christ, Lola, you plumb near give me a heart attack! What is it?!

PEARL: My bowels won't take that kind of shock, Lola. I swear
they won't.

MA: There's another one!

LESTER: What?

MA: Water bugs. I got the biggest ones in the state. I swear to
you they's crossed between a snappin' turtle and a jackass,
'cause I don't know nothing in tarnation that can stand these
number nines of mine, 'cept them bugs. Well, the place is
yours. I ain't had time to do much cleaning . . . as usual.

LESTER: As tired as I am I could sleep on a bed of rocks. I been
up all night for the past two nights nursing poor Pearl's condition. With a big trial comin' up in the mornin', I gotta get
some sleep.

MA: Big trial?

LESTER: Some damn foreigner . . . but it'll all come out in the
wash.

MA: I tell you outright, Judge Simmons, it ain't often we get
important guests like you and the missus stopping in.

PEARL: Could we get some rest now? I'm feeling powerful sick.

MA (*Whispering to* LESTER):   Is the missus in a family way?

LESTER: Which room . . . please?

MA: Is it your time of the month, honey? I got vinegar and . . .

PEARL: A bed, please. I've had diarrhea for two days.

MA: Second room on the left. Straight back. I'll see to your
horse and wagon.

(*We hear an owl's hoot*)

That owl hootin' like he's hoarse. Means either rain . . . or snow.

LESTER: In August?

MA: If it's God's will. If you have to go to the outhouse, there's plenty newspaper and a Sears catalogue already out there. (*Exits*)

PEARL: My Lord, this place is just a bug-infested dump. If this storm wasn't coming up, we could've made Baton Rouge.

LESTER: It was either here or the back of the wagon. And for God's sake don't tell anybody we stayed here. Knowing this old moonshine-making wench, the word'll be all around the parish by sunup. We should have left home earlier.

PEARL: Lester, I don't care 'bout your reputation. Not when I'm about to vomit.

> (PEARL *runs from the room. We hear her gagging in the bedroom as thunder rolls and lightning flashes.* LESTER *takes a lamp and exits to the bedroom. As we hear the sound of a wagon driving up,* PEARL *screams*)

(*Offstage*) Shittt!!! Bedbugs!

TATE (*Offstage*):   Whoa! We rest here for the night.

> (TATE *enters with* BUSHKIN, LILLY, *and* KITTY. TATE *has a pistol on his side and* BUSHKIN *is in handcuffs.* LILLY *and* KITTY *carry a cloth suitcase*)

LILLY: I tell you I come from Charleston aristocracy and I detest this treatment, you bag of cow dung!

KITTY: We boog-wa-zees, you no-count piece of white trash. Tell him, Alex.

BUSHKIN: Ladies, please.

TATE: Ladies? Anytime two women are married to the same man at the same time, we call them whores down here.

BUSHKIN: I'll face your judge, Mr. Tate, and force him to strike from the record that archaic law . . . a man can have only one wife. I'm from a long line of fighting Russians and . . .

TATE: I don't give a shit if you from a long line of rattlesnakes. You gonna be facing the hanging judge. The meanest son of a bitch to ever put on a black robe. Hates everybody including his own mama. Gave his baby brother twenty years for stealing. When he gits through with you . . . we'll see 'bout your fancy words and highfalutin ways.

KITTY: His baby brother. His . . .

TATE: This is Ma Lola's place. We stay here for the night. I'll be in the barn watching 'case you get any ideas 'bout trying to beat the odds with them gators. If you run, I'll kill you. You know I will. (*Exits*)

LILLY: He smells like horses. And I seen him rubbing one of them mares we come on in a very familiar way.

(BUSHKIN *looks to see if* TATE *is gone. He comes back*)

BUSHKIN: You two are the dumbest, imbecilic, moronic . . .

KITTY: Don't you be using no fancy Russian words on me, Alex.

LILLY: It was her fault!

BUSHKIN: It was both your faults. I should have left you both in that sporting house in Charleston.

LILLY: You . . . you said you loved us both.

KITTY: You got no choice now. You married us. I got my papers to prove it.

LILLY: Me, too.

BUSHKIN: You two were in charge of the maps. How could I navigate the boat, read the maps, fuel the engine . . . I told you Utah. We could live together as man and wives in *Utah.*

KITTY: I thought it was Utah. I didn't know it was Louisiana! We shouldn't have stopped in that town for supplies.

BUSHKIN: What were we supposed to eat? The bark from trees?

KITTY: If you was half a man, you woulda caught us some rabbits to eat.

BUSHKIN: With my bare hands?

KITTY: My daddy did it.

BUSHKIN (*Engrossed in his own thoughts*):   My oldest brother, Peter . . . Peter can kill with his bare hands. Peter always had blood under his fingernails. When we were young my father would take us on hunts. For geese. Peter would wait very patiently near the pond. When the geese came, the sky would be black from their wings. They would light down. Suddenly Peter would pounce upon a poor unsuspecting bird! And as we all watched, he would break the poor bird's neck. And while the bird was still alive, Peter would pluck the feathers from its body as the poor thing screamed in pain. He would just pluck and laugh. Now it's my neck that he wants to break.

LILLY: He done flipped out if you ask me!

BUSHKIN: Tate, my God. Maybe Tate's from the party. They sent Tate to kill me. No, no, no, no . . .

KITTY: Alex, Alex, man, you got to get a grip on yourself!

BUSHKIN: Communist bastards. Long live the bourgeoisie! Long
live—

LILLY: You just full of shit. Why don't you stop this play-acting
and get us out of this fix? How the hell did I ever let you
convince me you was a rich Russian prince?

> (*As* BUSHKIN *is about to enter the house,* MA *enters from stage
> right.* MA *has been in the barn talking to* TATE. MA *knows who*
> BUSHKIN, LILLY, *and* KITTY *are.* MA *gives* BUSHKIN *a disgusted
> look and enters the living room ahead of him. Lights come up to
> full on the living room as* BUSHKIN *enters behind* MA)

Who the hell are . . .

MA: You low-life, Godless things. Ain't y'all got one lick of
common decency? Tate told me all about it. You ought to read
your Bible. It speaks against what you're doing. And these two
tramps. These harlots!

KITTY (*Standing*):   Now just a damn minit!

MA: Don't you bull up against me, girl, or I'll wear this furni-
ture out with your hide. (*To* KITTY) Sit down. (KITTY *sits*) I never
thought I'd see the day when my dear, sweet home would be
shamed by your kind of horse manure. I can smell the stench
clean out in the yard.

BUSHKIN: Madam, it's obvious you have a limited command of
the English language, so I'll just pretend we aren't having this
conversation.

MA: You kin pretend anything you want. But the judge's gonna
hang you. He's a God-fearing man that hates Germans and
fornicators. And from what I hear from Tate, you might be
both.

BUSHKIN: I'm not Ger— Never mind.

MA: I got my buggy hitched up. I'm sleeping over to my sister's place tonight. The state pays me to put folks up traveling to court. That includes the likes of you. But I don't have to sleep under the same roof with you. And you'd better not get in my beds. You sleep out here. On the floor, on the ceiling, I don't care. Get in my beds and I'll shoot you.

BUSHKIN: Thank you for your strong sense of justice and fair play, madam.

(MA *exits*)

Imbeciles, barbarians. I hate these mutants they call Southerners. But I'll live. Do you hear me, Peter? You'll never find me. Never. Ladies, never listen to your older brother, especially when he's the only one entrusted to run the family estate. You will lose every time. Lenin, my dear Kitty, has a wretched philosophy, and he uses men like Peter. And my dear, dear Lilly, I'm absolutely horrified that my family can no longer summer at St. Petersburg. They've taken the Baltic from me, too.

LILLY: Alex, you the sweetest-talking man I ever heard. Now most of it I know ain't worth two cents. But you got one more silver tongue in this world. You talked me out of sexual favors that I normally charge for. For you it was free.

KITTY: Done it to me, too.

LILLY: Oh God, you can talk about the moon and the stars so pretty that my garter belt will just melt right before my eyes.

(*Suddenly* PEARL *runs through the room in her bathrobe.* PEARL *has a handful of newspapers*)

PEARL: The outhouse! Please let me make the outhouse! Don't stop me! Don't stop me!

(PEARL *exits through the front door.* LESTER *enters half asleep as* PEARL *exits*)

LESTER: Watch out for black widow spiders, honey! That toilet seat's rickety! It's my destiny never to sleep again as long as I live on earth. (*Sees* BUSHKIN, KITTY, *and* LILLY) Who the kingdom come are you?

BUSHKIN: I'm Alex Bushkin, good sir, and these are . . . this is my wife Kitty and this is Lilly . . . a friend of the family. Yes, a dear friend.

LESTER: I'm Lester Simmons. That blur that just run through here was my wife, Pearl.

BUSHKIN: I heard her say something about another house.

LESTER: Outhouse. Ma Lola don't have no inside relief facilities.

KITTY: Wonderful.

LESTER: She's had stomach cramps something terrible for the past two days. God, please let me go to sleep. Cure my Pearl so I can get a decent night's rest.

BUSHKIN: Poor dear. I'm a doctor of sorts. Maybe I can do something for her. A remedy.

LILLY: Stay out of it, Alex. You're no . . .

(PEARL *slowly drags herself back in and sits in a rocker*)

PEARL: I'm gonna die this time, Lester. I know I'm gonna die.

(BUSHKIN *goes to his suitcase and brings out a bottle of medicine*)

BUSHKIN: I know stomach remedy, sir. My mother was from Georgia.

PEARL: So is mine. Atlanta.

BUSHKIN: No, no. On the Black Sea. In Caucasia . . . in . . . never mind. Here. Drink.

(PEARL *drinks from* BUSHKIN's *bottle of medicine*)

PEARL: It's slimy.

BUSHKIN: It works.

PEARL: I hope so. Ain't much of my innards left.

LESTER: Thanks for the medicine, Mr. Bushkin.

BUSHKIN (*Looking at* PEARL): My pleasure. Any flower will bloom and stand tall and fragrant like the majestic rose, given the proper nourishment and . . . remedy.

PEARL: You talking 'bout me?

LILLY: He's got a cure for everything. 'Cept a noose.

BUSHKIN: I don't have one for a lonely disenfranchised exile whose inhabitancy is now a foreign Southern, mosquito- and alligator-infested shore. Deprived of his homeland by Lenin and the Marxist . . . and oh, yes . . . his own dear brother.

> (PEARL *is now absorbed in* BUSHKIN'*s every word.* PEARL *looks at* BUSHKIN *with a lover's eyes.* LESTER *has fallen asleep standing up*)

His own brother who wanted power and position in the party so badly, being so seduced by this antibourgeois philosophy that he sacrificed the family's wealth. To the disenfranchisement of the poor foreigner! Fuck the Bolsheviks! Drink up!

PEARL: Good Lord! I wish Lester would talk to me like that. That was just marvelous, Mr. Bushkin.

KITTY (*Pointing to* LESTER): Do Lester always sleep standing up?

> (*Pause.* PEARL *is looking at* BUSHKIN)

Well do he?

PEARL: Who, what, oh . . . yes.

LILLY: Looks like your hands is full tending to *your own* husband.

PEARL (*Shaking* LESTER):   Lester. Come on, honey. Wake up.

LESTER (*Waking up*):   Oh no, honey. Not again. I jest closed my eyes. You got to go again?

PEARL: Let's go to bed.

> (PEARL *leads* LESTER *out of the living room as her eyes are locked into* BUSHKIN'S. PEARL *and* LESTER *exit to their bedroom*)

LILLY: That wench's got eyes for you, Alex.

BUSHKIN: Nonsense.

KITTY: She can do whatever she wants with her eyes. I'm gonna close mine and get some sleep. If those rednecks gonna hang us, I don't want to die with bags under my eyes.

> (KITTY *lies down on the floor to sleep.* LILLY *lies on the couch*)

LILLY: Guess I shouldda made me out a will.

> (*There is silence as* BUSHKIN *paces the floor*)

BUSHKIN: Think, Alexis. Think. There's got to be a way out of here. (*Goes to the window. He sees* TATE *standing guard.* BUSHKIN *leaves the window. Suddenly* PEARL *bolts out of the bedroom on her way to the outhouse*)

PEARL: Tell my husband . . . I died . . . on the toilet seat. Lester!

> (PEARL *screams and* LESTER *hears the scream. Again he is awakened.* LESTER *slowly enters the living room.* KITTY *and* LILLY *are startled by* PEARL'S *scream*)

LILLY: The hell's going on?

BUSHKIN: My medicine worked.

KITTY: It did?

LESTER: It didn't! My wife's still got diarrhea.

BUSHKIN: But you said . . . she had stomach cramps.

LESTER: She do. Can't you see she do?

BUSHKIN: I . . . I treated her for . . . constipation.

LESTER: You what?

BUSHKIN: I . . . I . . . I gave her castor oil.

LESTER: You donkey's ass! You done killed my wife. (*Runs from the room to join* PEARL *at the outhouse*)

BUSHKIN: I'm cursed. Cursed! (*Looking toward heaven*) Am I never going to have good luck? Some good luck, please! Everything I touch just . . . dies. (*Runs to the window*) I know they're coming to kill me. They won't find me down here. No Russian in his right mind would travel this far south. But I must keep running . . . just in case.

> (LILLY *and* KITTY *lie down to sleep.* BUSHKIN *turns a quart bottle of vodka to his head. He runs over to the window and he looks out. He sees* LESTER *talking to* TATE. BUSHKIN *whispers to himself*)

He . . . he's talking to Tate! (*Leaves the window*) He knows. He knows about my wives. He knows who I am! How could he? Tate doesn't even know who I really am. (*Pauses, thinking. Talking quietly*) That's it. It's confirmed. The proletariat anarchist false leadership has sent Lester and Tate . . . to assassinate me. Pretend you don't know who he is when he comes back in and . . . beg for your life.

> (LESTER *slowly enters the house. He stops but doesn't look at* BUSHKIN. *Silence.* LESTER *has changed. He's now fully awake and there is menace in his voice*)

LESTER: Evil always overtakes me when the sky gets dark and cloudy. Thunder and lightning but no rain.

(*Silence*)

BUSHKIN (*Whispering aside*):   He's going to strike me. I can feel it. Delay the strike. Diverge. Diverge. (*To* LESTER) Yes . . . yes, Mr. Simmons. It does look like we're in for a rough storm.

LESTER: No. Sky's clear as a bell. Stars as bright as Aunt Flossie's gold teeth. Wolf moon, full and silvery.

> (*Silence.* LESTER *continues to act mysterious, not looking at* BUSHKIN)

BUSHKIN: How . . . how's your wife . . . doing?

LESTER: Thanks to you, Mr. Bushkin, she's got to sleep sittin' on that toilet seat. I throwed a blanket over her . . . kissed her . . . due to space and the condition of the air, we both couldn't occupy Ma Lola's exterior convenience at the same time. But I'll check on her from time to time.

BUSHKIN: Sir. I'm sorry about the wrong remedy. I was only trying to help. I . . .

> (KITTY *and* LILLY *sit up*)

LILLY (*To* BUSHKIN):   I told you to stay out of it.

LESTER: Oh, that's all right. It'll all come out in the wash.

BUSHKIN: The wash? Would you care for a drink? I . . . I've had more than my share. I'm starting to think dangerous thoughts. The liquid spirits are like that, you know.

LESTER: So is the ones made of flesh, you know. (*Looks at* BUSHKIN *and drinks from the bottle. Pause*)

BUSHKIN: Sir . . . have you been sent by the communists . . . to assassinate me?

LESTER: You got a dark, dark soul. So eat up with guilt and damnation that you think every shadow is the hangman's noose.

LILLY: And how would your soul feel if you had watched your brother pulling the bloody feathers from live gooses? And them damn things howling and screaming all over Russia from pain.

(*Pause*)

BUSHKIN: What did Tate tell you?

LESTER: Everything. You know we never stop here at Ma Lola's. That storm forcing us to stop here. Then it don't storm. You being here at the same time. It was divine intervention that brought us together. For what purpose, do you suppose?

BUSHKIN: Murder.

LESTER: No. Something higher than that. Judgment. You are a low, low, low, devil-infested, blasphemous bastard, Mr. Bushkin! Defying all of the natural laws of God and marrying two women! Bringing those harlots among the clean, chaste, undefiled people of this parish. What kind of heathen does that? One that should be punished! Flung out from among us! You're the devil! But we'll strike you down! Devil! Just fornicating all over our parish!

BUSHKIN: No, no, no! Listen to me, please. Lester, I can see that you're a compassionate, reasonable man.

LESTER: I been called worse.

BUSHKIN: You get angry. You lash out. That's good. It means you have conviction. Moral conviction.

LESTER: Boy, don't you talk to me 'bout morals. You one of them Mor-mons, ain't you?

BUSHKIN: I'm a Russian landowner.

LESTER: I'm John the Baptist.

BUSHKIN: It's true. I'm stranded here in this country. As you may have read . . . you *can* read, can't you?

LESTER: You'll know soon enough.

> (LILLY *and* KITTY *go to the window and look out. From the window we can see the sinister shadow of* TATE, *watching the house.* BUSHKIN *is now talking with the serious conviction of a man about to die, as he pleads to* LESTER *for help.* TATE'*s shadow disappears from the window*)

BUSHKIN: Mr. Simmons, I'm on my way to face the hanging judge. A satanic man who's probably full of ignorance, hatred, and no concern for justice. I'm frightened . . . I'm desperate, Mr. Simmons. I need help. If I'm guilty of anything . . . which I'm not . . . it's the desire to live and see my country liberated from the communists. I no longer have a family to go back to. My oldest brother sold out to the Bolsheviks. Giving away to a bad, bad system all that we've worked for. They asked me to come home. "Join the party. There is a place for you, Alexis." I didn't go back. My father denounced the party. He's dead. My mother denounced . . . she's dead. I'm the only other heir left. And I know they want me dead. I have been running in fear of my life for the past year since they came to power. I don't want to be sent back. I can fight them better here. I did marry two wives. I was going to Utah to live as a Mormon. But not as an evil man. But a man determined to live and liberate his country. Who would ever suspect me as being Alexis Bushkenov in Utah, with two wives? No honest, respectable Russian would do that. I was buying time.

LESTER: Then you were using those poor, innocent little harlot angels . . . as a disguise!

BUSHKIN: Angels of mercy, Mr. Simmons. They are being used for a glorious cause.

LESTER: Well, least you ain't one of them Kaiser Germans.

BUSHKIN: I denounce the Kaiser and I praise democracy's victorious victory in the Great War. (*Takes a drink*) Salud!

(LESTER *is caught up in the moment*)

LILLY (*At the window*):   Tate's disappeared.

LESTER: Yes, yes. Mine eyes have seen the glory! Sal-lud! (*Drinks. Pause*) You telling me the truth?

BUSHKIN: Yes, I am. And since we've been married . . . the ladies and I . . . we've never had sexual intercourse. Thanks to jealousy. I did pay for their sexual favors when they worked the Scarlet Garter in Charleston. But I swear to you, oh righteous sir . . . we never fornicated in this parish. (*Pause*) Please. Please help us. I don't want to die. Hanging is the worst. Please?

LESTER: I'll think on it.

BUSHKIN: I don't have a lot of time. When Tate comes for us . . . it's the end.

(*Silence as the two men look at each other.* LESTER *exits to his bedroom. After several beats,* PEARL *walks in zombielike.* PEARL *looks straight ahead*)

How . . . how do you feel?

PEARL: My behind's chafed beyond recognition. Musta been the newspaper print. Sears is usually softer, too.

(*Exits to her bedroom*)

BUSHKIN: If this is a bad dream, it's gone on far too long. That's it. Close my eyes and scream . . . wake up! Wake up! Wake . . . up!

(MA LOLA *and* TATE *enter.* MA LOLA *is holding a shotgun.* TATE *is carrying a hangman's rope*)

What . . . what are you doing? You can't do . . .

MA: Yes, we can. We ain't got to take you all the way to Baton Rouge. The judge sent Tate to get me over at my sister's. He wanted an impartial witness. Even though it's one hour 'fore rooster crow, the news sprung me wide awake.

TATE: You done been tried and we got the tree waiting.

BUSHKIN: We haven't been tried! What you're doing is illegal! We are entitled to a trial before a judge.

(LESTER *enters dressed in a black judge's robe.* PEARL *enters behind him*)

TATE: All rise. Judge Lester A. Simmons presiding.

BUSHKIN: You? You're the hanging judge? The one we're . . .

LILLY: Shit.

KITTY: Shit. Shit.

TATE: Will the accused please be seated?

KITTY: That's us, I reckon.

(BUSHKIN, KITTY, *and* LILLY *sit*)

LESTER: Will Alexis Bushkenov please rise.

(BUSHKIN *stands*)

BUSHKIN: Lester . . . Sorry. Your Honor. You haven't given us a fair trial.

LESTER: I've been trying you all night. Twenty years they've called me a hangman. I only listen to legal facts. The law. The law is the hangman. I'm only the administrator of the law and justice. I figured that I'd try a different tactic tonight, since fate had consciously thrown the judge and the accused into this strange arena of justice. I find judging with the heart a mite more interesting than judging with the legal facts. I see standing and sitting before me three of earth's lowest dogs. Driven by demons into sin and fornication. But . . . they're not Germans. This man is a liar and a deceiver, but . . . he loves democracy and he hates the Kaiser. He's given to strong drink, but . . . he's considerate of these two whores. And, yes, my darling wife, who he thought to be constipated. He's ignorant, I'll admit, but that's not his fault. He comes from a backward country of Russian infidels. May God have mercy on their souls and may they burn in hell. Until I met the accused, I'd never seen a human being grovel so and crawl on his belly, eyes filled with tears and begging for mercy. It was a beautiful sight. He has a mission in life which this court finds honorable and Christian. And he's convinced the court that he's not fornicated within the confines of this parish. (*Pause*) I ain't had a good hanging in twenty-two days.

TATE: Sir, you ain't thinking 'bout lettin' these snakes go, are you? I spent good time fixin' this noose, judge. You can't cheat me like that.

MA: We need a good hanging, Your Honor.

LESTER: I suppose I'm gettin' too soft for the job. Court . . . adjourned.

BUSHKIN: Thank you, sir! Thank you! From the bottom of my heart. Thank you! May I kiss your boots?

LESTER: If I catch you and these two buzzard baits in Louisiana again, well, I'll just kill you on sight. No trial.

BUSHKIN: Oh, no. Never again, sir. Never. (*Looks at* KITTY *and* LILLY)

LILLY: Never.

KITTY: In life. I promise on all that's sacred.

(LESTER *exits*. PEARL *looks back at* BUSHKIN. *Then she exits*)

TATE (*Disappointedly*):   I'm going . . . I don't know. Maybe I'll leave Louisiana altogether. Go where people believe in justice. Goodbye, Ma. I shore wanted to see somebody die. (*Exits*)

MA: I'm gonna burn my house down to the ground as a sacrifice to the defiling of the Holy Covenant.

BUSHKIN: I can assure you, my lady, we're not that important.

MA: Never thought I'd see the day Lester'd git soft in the head. Broke my heart, Lester. I'm gonna spend my last days at my sister's.

KITTY: What we gonna do now?

BUSHKIN: We are man and wives, but if you want to break the vows, I'll understand.

KITTY: Break . . . man, it was you who was playing them games. I don't want to break no vows. Do you know how hard a good, intelligent man is to come by? You the catch of the year!

LILLY: I'll be headin' back to South Carolina.

BUSHKIN: You'll be heading to Utah with your husband. Unless . . . well . . . you just have to.

LILLY: Utah'd be more interesting, although I know I'm gonna have to scratch Kitty's eyes out.

KITTY: Try it!

BUSHKIN: Ladies . . . ladies. Let's just get our bag and leave. Fast!

KITTY: We already packed. I'll git the bag.

LILLY: I'll help.

(*As* BUSHKIN *is preparing to leave,* PEARL *tiptoes into the room with her suitcase. In the distance we hear a rooster crowing in the dawn*)

KITTY: What you sniffing around for?

BUSHKIN: Mrs. Simmons.

PEARL: Call me Pearl. I'm going with ya.

BUSHKIN: You what?! Your husband will . . .

PEARL: Sleep till noon. It's 'bout daylight now. So we'll git a big head start on him. We'll just git on your boat and head out.

BUSHKIN: But why?

PEARL: Well . . . both our families from Georgia. And I believe in the bond of names. No matter how different the location on earth. It's a sign. You was sent as a sign to me and . . . I want to help you retake Russia. I do.

BUSHKIN: But you can't go with us . . .

PEARL: You ain't got no choice. If I tell my husband you asked me for favors of my flesh, ain't *nobody* gonna leave.

BUSHKIN: You wouldn't.

PEARL: The hell I won't. I am sick and tired of this place, and you my last hope. And I want to be one of your *wives* . . . comrade!

BUSHKIN: No!

KITTY/LILLY: What?

LILLY: The hell you will. Me and Kitty ain't sharing this man!

BUSHKIN (*To* LILLY):   Ssssh! You want to wake up the judge? Mrs. Simmons, what you're doing is called *blackmail*.

PEARL: I know what it's called. But you done messed around and made me fall in love with you. I never heard a man talk as sweet as you in my entire life. You make this majestic rose blossom just wilt under your power.

KITTY: Cactus plant, is more like it.

BUSHKIN (*To* KITTY *and* LILLY):   We don't have a choice. (*To* PEARL) You want to be my . . .

PEARL: Wife! (*Picks up her bag and tiptoes out the door*)

BUSHKIN/LILLY/KITTY (*To the audience*):   Three?!

The Talking Dog

by

JOHN GUARE

A bare stage. White.

F: Hang-gliding!

M: Hang-gliding.

F: I don't understand anything *about* hang-gliding!

M: You wear this harness—

F: You don't understand—

M: You insert yourself into the machine—

F: I am a complete coward—

M: The wings—the sails—the structure takes care of every-
    thing—

F: All I have to do is jump off the mountain. Look at it down
    there! It's miles—don't get too close! Watch out for the edge!
    Oh dear God, I am not religious and I am praying! You have
    me praying! This goddam mountain—

M: This is not a mountain.

F: That's right. Don't pay any attention to my nosebleed or the thin air or the birds flying below us—the birds have nosebleeds!

M: This is the Catskills.

F: The Catskills *are* mountains. The Catskills are not Death Valley turned upside down. The Catskills are not the Gobi Desert.

M: The Alps are mountains. The Himalayas are mountains.

F: And the Catskills—

M: —are the Catskills. You just strap on your machine and step over the edge.

F: Be careful!

M: Feel the air. The wind. The purity. Breathe deep!

F: And you like to do this?

M: It's what you said about courage.

F: Courage.

M: We have to give ourselves tests of courage all the time to grow, to know we're progressing.

F: Stepping off a mountain is not a progression. Except one way. The air is too thin here. I want to be taken down. By a car. On a road.

M: Don't you want to appear worthwhile to yourself? Don't you want to know you're strong? That you have the strength for life? You have to grow, and the best way to grow—

F: Is not to jump off a mountain—

M: Is by a simple act of courage. And you're protected. You stretch out in the machine. These ropes operate the struts, the wings. You actually control the wind. Mastery over nature! You control the invisible! That which is invisible holds you up. It is impossible to plummet. You are safer in this glider than you are, say, crossing Fifth Avenue. The wind catches you, supports you, welcomes you. A baby could be put in this and glide to earth as safely as Moses drifting in the bulrushes.

F: If I had a baby, I would not let it hang-glide. Moses or not.

M (*Sings lightly, seductively*):   Rockabye baby
In the tree top
When the wind blows
The cradle will rock—

F: The cradle will *drop*. Drop rhymes with top. Down will come baby, cradle, and all—

M: Just strap the harness on.

(HANG-GLIDER #1 *in his bright-colored jumpsuit comes to* HER. HANG-GLIDER *stands waiting, expectantly, good-natured, arms outstretched, welcoming, wearing black-lensed goggles.* SHE *backs away.* SHE *looks over the edge*)

F: I land down there?

M: You land down there.

F: How long?

M: Does it take?

F: How long does it take?

M: It can be over in a few minutes.

F: No!

M: Or if you're good—

F: I want to be good.

M: It can take . . . oh, you can prolong it, prolong the flight, extend the voyage for as long as you can keep control, feel the desire, control the wind, find new bits of current. Slow. Slow. Slow.

F: What's the longest you've ever stayed up?

M: Once—almost an hour.

F: An hour!

M: Generally thirty minutes.

F: You're good.

M: I'm good.

F: Courage.

M: Courage.

F: Were you afraid at first?

M: Everybody is.

F: I want to be strong.

M: Then just do it. You're not alone. Look down there.

F: Other people leaping off the cliffs. Filling the air.

M: This is the hang-gliding capital of the world.

F: I don't see anybody plunging down.

M: They gave you the lesson.

F: We paid the money.

M: I'll fly right beside you.

F: The wind is so high.

M (*Testing the wind*):   If it wasn't—ahh, then I'd be worried.

F: And you're not frightened.

M: Just that little edge in the stomach—that one frightened edge to conquer.

F: We strap ourselves in and go?

M: Yes.

> (SHE *adjusts her harness.* SHE *stands with her back to* HANG-GLIDER #1. HANG-GLIDER *attaches her harness to the strap on his chest.* HANG-GLIDER *lifts* HER. SHE *wraps her legs around* HANG-GLIDER's *waist and extends her arms out in front of her, her back arched, her stomach parallel to the ground.*
> M *puts on his helmet.* HE *puts her helmet on her head and kisses her hands, which* SHE *puts into a prayer position.*
> HANG-GLIDER #2 *appears in his brightly colored jumpsuit and black goggles.* M *quickly and expertly adjusts his straps onto* HANG-GLIDER's *chest.* HANG-GLIDER #2 *hikes up* M, *who wraps his legs around* HANG-GLIDER's *waist, and confidently stretches out his arms, his back arched, his stomach parallel to the ground.* THE HANG-GLIDERS *walk their two passengers to the back of the playing area.* M *and* F *stand side by side.* HE *raises his hand*)

M: Ten.

F: Nine.

M: Eight.

F: Oh dear God.

M: EIGHT.

F: Seven.

M: Six.

F: Five.

M: Four.

F: I can't.

M: FOUR.

F: Three.

M: Two.

F: One.

> (*And* THEY *step forward, their arms extended like wings. The
> sound of wind.* SHE *screams.* THEY *crisscross each other, swooping
> around the stage, up, down, free. Delight*)

I'm doing it! I am not believing this! I am doing, actually
doing, look at me doing this! Do you see me?

M: I.
     Love.
     You.

> (F *is silent for a moment, not sure of what she's heard.* SHE *lifts
> off her helmet and cranes her head.* M *signals her wildly to put
> her helmet back on, which she does.*
> THE HANG-GLIDERS *bring them to earth, detaching their har-
> nesses.* HE *rolls and rolls over and over and jumps up vigorously,
> breathing heavily, excitedly, pulling off his helmet.* F *is ex-
> hausted.* SHE *sits in a heap, strangely troubled*)

Did—did you like it?

F (*Deep breaths*):   I've never been more scared—that's a fact. I'm
shaking. My breath. I'm afraid to feel my pulse.

M: Your pulse is fine.

F: You didn't tell me I'd have to use all my muscles. The power
in the wind. It's not a free ride. There's no ground below you.
The psychic shock. I'm in a sweat. The wind is so powerful.

M: Did you think you'd just move your pinky one way and the wind does this and you flick your wrist the other and the wind does that? All the reading. Lessons. Nothing prepares you for the power.

F: Or the sounds.

M: The sounds?

F: I thought I heard something.

M: Heard what?

F: Could—could we try it again?

> (SHE *signals.* THE HANG-GLIDERS *reappear*)

M: I thought you didn't like it. The absence of earth. No terra firma. Only terror . . .

F: But if you did it with me . . .

> (SHE *looks at him.* THEY *put on their helmets. Facing each other,* THEY *attach themselves to* THE HANG-GLIDERS *once more, and go to the back of the playing area.*
> THEY *step forward.* THEY *swoop through space. The sound of the wind.* THEY *crisscross back and forth, their arms extended*)

M: I.
Love.
You.

> (SHE *looks up eagerly.* THEY *land.* SHE *rolls over this time more confidently.* SHE *leaps up*)

F: Again!

M: There's a long line. There's rentals. It's by the hour.

F: Again. Again. Again. Again. Again.

M: There's money.

F: Again.

M: There's time. I have to get back to work.

F: Again.

M: You have to get back to work.

F: When can we do it again?

> (SHE *puts on her helmet.* HE *puts on his helmet.* THEY *attach themselves to their* HANG-GLIDERS *and swoop over the stage, whooping joyously*)

M: I.
Love.
You.

> (THEY *land on earth.* SHE *pulls off her helmet and looks at him expectantly*)

Yes?

F: Don't you want to say—something?

M: Say something? Like what?

> (SHE *steps back.* SHE *studies him.* HE *stands there smiling, puzzled.* HE *and* HANG-GLIDER #2 *back away*)

Like what?

> (SHE *is alone with* HANG-GLIDER #1. SHE *waits expectantly, checking her watch.* SHE *puts on her helmet.* SHE *attaches herself to* HANG-GLIDER #1, *goes to the back of the playing area, and steps forward, her arms outstretched in space.* SHE *glides.* HE *watches secretly, stifling laughter.* SHE *listens. Silence.* SHE *lands.* M *runs out to her*)

Solo!

F: Where were you?

M: Got stuck in traffic.

F: I waited. Come up with me?

M: I hurt my knee.

F: You didn't hurt your knee.

M: I can't go up. What? Do you think I'm joking? I hurt my knee. The Catskills are the home of the Borscht Belt comedians, but I'm no Catskill comic. I hurt my knee.

F: Are you serious?

M: Of course I'm serious. Why wouldn't I be serious?

F: Do you ever hear voices?

M: Like Joan of Arc? Joan of Arc of the Catskills? Now that's funny.

F: Do you believe Nature ever talks to us?

M: Nature ever talks to us?

F: Nature ever breaks its silence and speaks to us?

M (*Stifling laughter*): What does Nature have to say to me?

F: To get us . . . to get us to join her.

M: Her?

F: I don't mean *Her* in a feminist way. I don't mean Her. But I don't really mean *Him*. Nature enlisting us, calling us to join— it's not *It*.

M: Pantheism?

F: Not pantheism because it's not God. I've never used the word "pantheism" in a sentence, so it's a shame it's not the right word, but it's more—

M: Songs like "The Breeze and I"? "I Talk to the Trees"?

F: No . . . maybe yes . . .

M: And what is Nature saying?

F: Don't you know?

M (*Stifling laughter*):   I just want to get this straight. Are you saying you have heard Nature speaking? This is very fascinating.

F: Have you ever heard it? That's all I'm asking.

M: Are you setting forth a theory or speaking about fact?

F: Could we go up for another ride?

M: My knee.

F: Your knee.

M: I'll hate it when winter comes and the snow and we can't do this.

F: Skiing?

M: Skiing's not the same. Gliding. The air. The height.

F: Just once more?

> (THE HANG-GLIDERS *lift* M *and* F *up and carry them around once more.* SHE *listens.* HE *is silent.* THEY *land.* THE HANG-GLIDERS *retreat*)

I guess . . . no, just a theory . . . a dopey . . .

M: Oh, theory. I'm not good on theory. I'm a reality kind of guy.

F: Yes. Reality.

M: I had—I don't know what makes me think of this—but I had this friend once who could train animals. She was a great trainer of anything animal. The *National Geographic* offered her lifetime contracts and unlimited expense accounts and introductions to safaris all over the world. And Viola had this Alaskan husky. White. Hairy. Blue glassy eyes of a wolf. And the

first time I went to her house to pick her up, I rang the door-
bell. The door opens and there is this great Alaskan husky
sitting down on its haunches, tail flapping away making this
thud thud thud on the hooked rug, and Fido puts up its
haunches and says (*Makes a growling noise like a hound baying*):

> I
> Love
> You

F: The husky talked?

M: Viola trained Fido—trained this Alaskan wolf—to turn its
growl into this sound:

> Hello
> I
> Love
> You

Well, Viola stepped around the door and flashed a flashbulb
taking my photo, the look of shock on my kisser. She loved to
take photos of people's faces when they heard this husky talk.

F: Why?

M: A joke. It made her very popular. People would come from
various nations to hear the dog talk.

> Hello
> I
> Love
> You

People would swear off alcohol and drugs or else take *up* alco-
hol and drugs. This dog would look at you with its vaguely
Oriental eyes of such intelligence and the growl
Hello
You'd think you'd gone over the hill . . . the edge . . . Don't
you think that's funny?

F: Well . . . she went to a lot of effort.

M: That was Viola.

F: What happened to Viola?

M: I don't know. The jungles. Talking alligators.

Hello

I

Lo—

I'm . . . I should tell you. I'm being transferred. Moving to another coast. Well, more towards the middle of the country. But a transfer. You really are terrific, how good you've become. It's really rewarding to see . . . and that sense of courage . . . that . . .

> (M *has backed offstage as* HE *talks and is gone.* F *sits by herself, at a loss.* M *appears at the back of the stage, tiptoeing on very quietly.* HE *calls out softly*)

I

Love

You

> (HE *stifles a laugh as* SHE *sits up, listening*)

I

Love

You

> (SHE *is amazed.* SHE *holds her arms out to infinity, smiling. The lights begin to fade on her.* HE *comes forward and speaks to us*)

So I moved away. Transferred to another city, but I always check into New York with the Sunday papers and I saw one Sunday not long ago that she—that she was engaged to some nerd. With a name like Casper. Or Rufus. Some stupid cretinous name. Or else she married him. That page where it's all weddings and engagements and plans for the future. That page. I don't envy Rufus. Or Casper. I mean, she was a—grew into a great hang-glider. Well, an adequate hang-glider, but I don't think she was too much in the sense of humor department. Poor Rufus. Poor Casper. Living with somebody who couldn't take a joke. This is years ago now . . . (*In his dog voice*)

> Hello
>
> I
>
> Love
>
> You

I mean, if I couldn't live with somebody like Viola—well, aside from her dog, Viola had no sense of humor whatsoever, but aside from that, I'd just as soon live alone as live with somebody who couldn't take a

> take a
>
> take a (M *imitates a broken record*)
>
> take a
>
> joke.

Rivkala's Ring

by

SPALDING GRAY

If there is something comforting—religious, if you want—about paranoia, there is still also antiparanoia, where nothing is connected to anything, a condition not many of us can bear for long.

—THOMAS PYNCHON

"Go, go, go," said the bird: "Human kind cannot bear very much reality."

—T. S. ELIOT

CHARACTERS

A PERSON

Now, just some thoughts about the staging of this. I see the character as a kind of manic-y paranoid person who's spinning off these kind of paranoid delusions, trying to make order out of a very frightening and chaotic existence. So I see it fashioned after my character, the character of Spalding Gray that I do in the monologues. And I suggest as a character study, for whoever's playing this, that they see the monologue *47 Beds,* which can be seen at the Lincoln Center Library for the Performing Arts. They'll set up a screen there in the video room if you call them. So that monologue should be observed as a kind of character study. Then, I see the set as quite simple. It's a series of very small surfaces, like, not even platforms—they're too small. They're two-by-two facets like a diamond so the person who's doing the monologue can't get any footing. They're shiny wood, like a wood floor. But he can never, it's always like he's . . . the heel's trying to get his footing. He or she, I don't know. And I guess it's a man, I see a man. And I also see him standing with a microphone, a roving microphone, like a phone on a wire. So that it's amplified. And he's like a stand-up comedian, but in no way working like one—it's reminiscent of one. And the character's barefoot, he's got white pants and one of those real bright Hawaiian-type California shirts. A flowery silk Hawaiian shirt.

And a man tan on his face. His arms look white. Nothing on that but his face is out of show tanning, or actual tan. And behind him, just to his right and about twelve feet back, is a big Venetian blind which is just extended and a little bit opened, and besides general lighting or specific light on him, there is moonlight, blue light that is seeping through the blinds, coming directly and very intense from backstage through that blind. And that's really simply the set, and it's a pretty direct delivery to the audience.

THE PERSON: The day the Chekhov short story arrived I saw my first missing child. On a milk carton. And found a drowned rat in our pool. The photo of the child barely left an impression; it was like any black-and-white photograph of any child anywhere. The more I studied the face, the more it broke up and blended into abstract dots; and besides, I hadn't seen any stray children in the neighborhood. I hadn't seen any children. For that matter, I hadn't seen any people either. There were plenty of houses, but no people. Renée and I were sub-letting in the Hollywood Hills just below the Hollywood sign. And all the Venetian blinds in all the houses were always closed. And everyone seemed deep dark inside, writing final drafts of their latest TV scripts. Our swimming pool was big-ger than our apartment. And much colder. It wasn't heated and we could only look at it and never go in.

Anyway, the particular morning the Chekhov short story ar-rived, I was on my way to fetch the mail when I noticed the drowned rat floating in among the eucalyptus leaves. The wind had blown wild the night before. A mighty Santa Ana had swept in under a full moon, turning everything upside down. Electricity was blown out and semitrailers were over-turned in the lowlands. I couldn't sleep. The wind came in and stirred me and reminded me so much, too much, of raw indifferent nature. The bare-boned breath of the desert whipping in over this crazy glitter town.

So maybe the rat had blown out of the palm tree. Joe, our upstairs neighbor, said that the rats lived in palm trees and that they often drowned in the pool because they were too stupid to use the steps. Or more like their little feet didn't go down that deep. Joe said that when the weather got real hot, all the various creatures came down early out of the Hollywood Hills to take a dip in the pool: coyotes, raccoons, and skunks—all sorts of stuff. And they had the good sense to use the steps of the pool, swim a few measured laps, and then jog back into the hills where they belonged. I pictured a possum in little Nike jogging shoes shaking off the water from his fur and jogging off toward the Hollywood sign.

But I couldn't help calling Renée's attention to this drowned rat—the way it hung there so suspended in the pool with his little legs dangling and his white whiskers out, fully suspended in the water—like it was still alive, or stuffed. Like Mr. Rat, you know, like Mr. Comic Book Rat. Mr. Unharmful Stuffed Rat. The way the water held those whiskers out made me call out to Renée: "Renée! Come quick, come quickly, you've got to see this!"

And she, having no idea what I was talking about, scurried out like a little kid. Scurried out barefoot with her hands clasped across her chest like this little excited kid. And then when she saw what it was, she started screaming and said, "Get it out! Get the net. Get it out!" She couldn't look at it.

It wasn't that I was trying to torture Renée. It was more like a piece of me was missing; the screaming part was missing. Like Renée always said, "I love you but you're a funny guy because you have a piece of your pie missing. Sometimes you don't react in a normal human way to stuff that needs a scream or a cry." And then she does it for me. So Renée completes me, you see. She makes up for the missing piece of the pie. I needed her to be upset about the rat. Then and only then could I toss that sad swollen rat body into the rotten palm leaves and have done with it.

There was another rat, come to think of it. There was another rat in our life in New York City just before we moved to Hollywood. But first, let me tell you what was happening out here just before the Chekhov story came.

Renée and I had just eaten at the Japanese place that night. I had become overly addicted to eating at the Sizzler. And Renée was probably right—it was no good for me. Because I have no boundaries. And so I never get any real satisfaction from those "all you can eat" places. I overdo it and don't get any satisfaction. I feel I have to try everything. And no one says "Stop" or "Pay me more." All the people are so fat. So Renée insisted that we go to this skinny Japanese place that she couldn't get into the week before because it was too crowded. But this time we got in. And it was like we had all of a sudden flown into Japan. I mean, we were the only non-Japanese in the place. And it was real crowded with all these Japanese-speaking Japanese and I felt real uneasy at first. I mean, I felt a little guilty about the bomb and all, even though I was only four years old when we dropped it. But still, I was from Rhode Island, which is still one of the few states in the U.S.A. which celebrates V-J day. But I started to relax a little after a few sakis and some beer and I must admit I felt better being in a place where the service of the food was under tight control. And it all came to us in little frames. And you had plenty of time to meditate on what you ate after you ate it. And lots of time to meditate before you ate. I mean, in short, it was all very controlled (and well framed).

When Renée and I left the restaurant the Santa Ana winds had already begun to blow and we went back to what we were calling home that month to watch our rented TV, which didn't get very good reception because of the Hollywood Hills. But anyway, the important thing (at least I think it was the important thing) was that I turned on the TV and there was this show about General MacArthur taking over Japan after World War II. I had no idea that this had happened. I mean, he became more powerful and more respected than the Emperor of Japan. And also he knew how to deal with the communists. He had all this super faith in democracy, so he just gave the communists total freedom. And they lost. They lost in the elections.

And I said, "Renée, Renée, look. Isn't it strange. Isn't it strange that we should have just eaten in a Japanese restaurant and now this is on TV?" I wanted to say "Jap" restaurant, but I corrected myself. "Look! When we come home and we find this on television—don't you think it's at all strange?"

She said no, she didn't think it was all that strange. She was thinking of other things and went to bed early.

I tried to go to bed after the MacArthur show but I couldn't sleep because of the wind and the full moon. And I got up to watch thé late news, which is for me a kind of homeopathic medicine. If I can't sleep because of anxiety, I seek a more anxious state outside of myself. And that is almost always the late news. And that particular night was as good as any other. It was, shall we say, consistent.

It all started with a local report from Laguna Beach with what seems to be an AIDS epidemic there. They had more cases of AIDS relative to the population than in any other city in the United States. And they were having a town meeting to discuss the problem. It was a real alarming sort of thing. This guy, I don't know whether he was a doctor or what, but he was talking about how the number of AIDS cases in the United States had doubled every nine months, and if it continued at that rate, and spread into the general population, that would mean in twelve years everyone in the United States will have been killed. In another twelve years, that's twenty-four years, the population of the world would have been killed ten times over.

Now this doctor-type guy went on to talk about these weird things which I thought were pretty far out for the late news. He said the job of our immune system was to tell the difference between what was itself and what was not itself. You know, to make frames—draw boundaries. And if the immune system gets overworked, it gets overaggressive in response. It gets all confused and the body begins to attack its own cells in a state of what they call "organic paranoia."

It's all led me to believe that eating at the Sizzler was bad because it fostered a lack of definition, a kind of dietary anarchy. Also, I felt that living in Hollywood was bad for the same reasons. Hollywood was the town where everyone came to proliferate their image. And I thought that cancer could be a common disease among movie stars because the image was proliferating out of control and their cells were reacting to that. But finally it all had to do with Russia, I was sure. With Russia or America's attitude toward Russia or Russia's attitude toward America. Just relationshipal problems, big superpowers. And I began to think we were all going to die because of Star Wars. Because that's a massive external defense and no one's putting money into internal body defense. The more that goes to protecting the outside, the less that goes to protecting the inside. External, internal—it's all the same. And also these doctor-type guys no longer know what a high-risk area is. You know, high-risk for AIDS. Everything is high-risk. You never know what the right or wrong place is. I mean, everyone is dying right after they're born, in the sense that we are all headed for an eventual death that will most likely last forever. And it's that "forever" that wipes me out. I mean, wipes me right out. When I think about "forever" it pushes me right out of the existing now because "forever" is so big that it crowds me out, out of the picture. And makes me disappear. And I don't know if or when I'm in a high-risk area for AIDS because it's all a big chain of events that has to be looked at in context from a big kind of overview. And who has that? Who has an overview, right? Because to be over it, to have an overview is to be outside of it. And no one can get out. We're all in too deep.

Well, during this whole report on AIDS, the AIDS epidemic in Laguna, I got up and took this big dose of folic acid, which is supposed to help hold your cell walls together. And while I was in the kitchen, this ad came on the TV for the Doggery Boutique. And it showed clips of this woman holding a poodle down in a Jacuzzi. The poodle looked very disturbed and was trying to get out, but it was helpless. I thought about the drowned rat in the pool and I got up to make some warm milk and take a big dose of L-Tryptophan, a natural tranquilizer made from turkey enzymes. A guy sold it to me in a health food store in Venice—I bought six jars of it on sale. He was a good salesman: He said, "Ever wonder why you want to go right to sleep after a big Christmas dinner?"

And that stopped me, because it was true. Thinking back over it, that was a major memory of Christmas and Thanksgiving. You know—sleeping. And I just thought it had to do with eating too much, and he said, "No, no, no, it had to do with L-Tryptophan in the turkey." Then he tried to sell me six jars of something. I can't remember the name of it. It was for aiding the memory. Um. And I told him I didn't want to remember anymore, it was too painful. That I just wanted to relax, and go out simple.

Then he starts on this whole rap how history not remembered is doomed to repeat itself.

And I fled from the store, only to pass this guy with a

shopping cart out on the street, and it was all filled with his possessions. And he calls out to me, saying, "Fifty dollars to bring democracy back to the United States!"

And that stops me. I mean, anyone who has the balls to ask for a fifty-dollar handout . . . well, anyway, I stopped and I say, "Tell me, when did democracy leave America?"

And he says, "Nineteen sixty-three, when the wealthy right wing paid for all those assassination plots."

And I listened because the guy started to make disturbing sense, until I asked him, "What can we do about this, I mean, where is the fifty dollars gonna go? And if I give you fifty dollars, where's it gonna go?"

And he says, "To organize the big July 22nd rally."

"Really? What rally?"

He says, "What's gonna save us all is that Christ and Moses are both coming back on July 22nd. Together they're coming back. What a team!"

I said, "Where's this all going to happen?"

"Right here!" he says. "On the beach of Venice. Where else could we hold that many people?"

So I said, "Okay, would fifty cents help?"

And he said, "Yeah, thanks. Anything, anything will help."

And just as we were talking, you know, about Jesus and Moses coming back, this real wasted bum, barefoot, an old hippie with a bandana wrapped around his head, comes wandering through and says, "Hey I'm Jesus, I'm Jesus Christ!"

And the guy with the shopping cart says, "Keep moving, Jack, don't bug me with that crazy shit!"

And I think: Where does it all stop? Where does it all begin? It's like panning for gold. But no one knows what the gold is anymore. I mean, that's what I said to Renée when we made up our minds to come out to Hollywood. I said, "That's where the gold is. That's where the money is. Just pretend we're pioneers. It's like panning for gold."

.   .   .

So we get this cheap flight out on Tower Air, and I'm feeling
real nervous because it's cheap. And I'm worried that the pilot
isn't getting paid enough money to make him satisfied, and so
he's in a rush and we're sitting there, and behind us are these
two dark, sensual ladies. And one of them moves in on a guy
in front of us because he's real cute. And he's got one of those
mod-punk haircuts that ends in a sort of long rattail that goes
out over his collar. And there's an empty seat next to him and
it looks like she's plying him with lines of coke. You know,
cocaine! And, I mean, she's just making little lines of cocaine
on the dinner tray, and after a few snorts, they disappear into
the toilet to join the mile-high club. And they're in there for a
long time and this long line begins to build up outside the
toilet. And I'm amazed and jealous that they don't seem to
care. Their pleasure is more important than anyone else's
needs. It must be the drug, I think. I rarely take the stuff; it's
too expensive, and too up and down––but I never say no to an
offered snort (which is rare).

The last time I had it was when my friend George came out to
visit from the West Coast. Oh, that was incredible that day.
That was the day we saw all that money blowing in the street.

Every time my friend George comes from the Coast for a
visit he wants to go with me to a place in New York where I
haven't been for a long time. I guess he wants us to be experi-
ential equals, you know, on equal ground. So this particular
spring day we wound up in the East Village, corner of 11th
and B, to be precise. And the vibes are pretty heavy; they're
as heavy as they've ever been. And George gets queasy because he's got two hundred dollars in cash in his pocket. And
he wants to move on and I say, "Let's go over to Surprising
SoHo." And we get there, and we're walking down West
Broadway, which is really crowded with all these tourists and
bridge and tunnel people. You know, wall-to-wall mink. And

the first scene that George and I come upon is this silver-gray Cadillac with chrome wheels. And it's talking. The car is talking, or rather, it's crying out, "BURGLAR! BURGLAR! BURGLAR! BURGLAR!" Over and over again, "BURGLAR! BURGLAR! BURGLAR!" And all these women in their minks and foxes are standing around staring at this car which is talking. And they're all looking at it as if to say, "Who, me? Who you calling a burglar? ME?!" And the car is just sitting there like this . . . you know, like this big accusatory metal beast, just sitting there going "BURGLAR! BURGLAR!"

So George and I take this all in and move on down a little farther to the corner of Spring Street and West Broadway, where we come upon this crowd of people all standing around in a circle looking down like they're looking into a great hole in the Earth. Like they're looking into El Dorado. Like the Earth has opened up and they're looking at this gold city. And one woman is crying out, "What shall we do? What shall we do!" And we get to the circle and look down and see green not gold, but green instead of gold. There's all this green money blowing in the wind in circles like leaves. I mean, there must have been a thousand dollars there! I saw some hundreds, lots of fifties, uncountable twenties. And all the people are standing around it. And it's blowing in circles. And not one person is going in for it—but George.

As soon as George sees that money he just follows his natural inclinations and he bends down and picks up a twenty. Just one twenty out of all that money, he just picks up one twenty.

And the woman who has been crying out, "What shall we do? What shall we do?" turns to him and says, "Oh, my God! What are you doing?"

And George looks right back at her and says, "You know what I'm doing." And we walk off down the street.

And as we're walking, I say, "George, why didn't you pick up a hundred? Why did you pick up a twenty?"

And he goes, "What? There were hundreds there?" And then he stops, looks back, and then he turns to me and says, "No. That would be greed, wouldn't it?" And then we move off down the street together.

Now I can't stop thinking about that money. It's become one of those "spots" that are forever marked in the city. No matter how much I try to be here now and see the spot for what it is, I can't get that blowing money out of my mind.

It's the same with the spot on North Moore and Greenwich where Renée and I saw the fresh body of a blond woman. She must have jumped just minutes before we rounded the corner. And it was such a nice day. It was spring and a Sunday. And the streets were empty and we saw these people standing around this blond body. She was so . . . dead. So there, but so not there. I mean, there wasn't one hint of life coming off of her. Her face was white like wax, in a puddle of blood. The blood flowed out from some opening, some crack somewhere that you couldn't see. And her whole body was sprawled in an impossible sprawl. A fix of wasted limbs nobody could imitate. And she had only jumped from the fifth-floor window. That's all! That's as high as the building was—just five stories.

Renée burst into tears and ran away. She had had bad luck with suicides in that neighborhood before. Just the past winter when she was going over to apply for an apartment at Independence Plaza, some woman jumped from about twenty stories up, bounced off a trash dumpster, and broke open at Renée's feet like an overripe watermelon. So I could understand why she didn't stick around.

I stuck around because I couldn't see it. I mean, at first it was so strange, I had to look hard so I could see it. And all the time there was this old woman who lived on the fourth floor of the building and she was standing over that body. And the face was so white. And the blond hair was so beautiful that I wanted to run my hands through it and cry. And the blood was so red, so crimson. How could someone else's death look so beautiful? I kept wondering. And this old woman was standing over the body. This old woman with a kind of shaky palsy. She was shaking all over and saying over and over again, "How could she have done it? She's so beautiful and young." And she doesn't even know who this dead body is! And the other people are talking about how the dead body was a woman who was just crashing there, just visiting. And she couldn't sleep, she was real upset. She had a rough night. And her friends had stayed up with her all night. They had done an all-night vigil to help her keep it together. And then around morning she seemed better and the friends had dozed off like Christ's disciples. You can't blame them. And she did it. She just jumped. And here was this old woman who felt from her side of the fence that beauty was enough to go on living for. You could just live for sheer beauty, physical beauty. Why would anyone who had that kind of beauty, who possessed that kind of beauty, why would they want to jump? She couldn't understand it.

I stayed and watched until the ambulance came. I wanted to see how they would deal with the body. Who would finally touch it. And how they would touch it. But no one touched it. The ambulance came and they had a stretcher that was like a scoop. The stretcher opened and then closed like a big mouth eating the body whole. It just scooped it up like this very, very dead thing that it was. And the blood stayed in a big puddle, and a gust of wind came off the river and blew a fine layer of city dirt over the blood and the blood turned a deep darker dirty red. And it left a stain that stayed for months. And now it's just the old dirty sidewalk again.

But every time I walk over it, I see that body. Just like I

see the money blowing every time I walk by that corner of Spring Street and West Broadway.

Anyway, a Sizzler ad comes on the TV and I realize why I'm addicted to Sizzler—they have such great ads. And the food looks so good. And they follow the ad with this outrageous story about a man, a photographer in Florida, who has gotten cancer of the eye. And I think: Oh my good Christ, that's enough! You know, just that: that's enough of the story right there. I mean, you could end it all right there. But they didn't. They went on to describe this horrible medical mistake. It turns out that in order to operate on his eye, they had to remove some of his spinal fluid to take some of the pressure off his eye. And instead of putting his spinal fluid back into his spine, they inject him with some sort of embalming fluid which just happened to be in the operating room in an unmarked bottle. And they end up embalming the patient. I mean, they turn him into a vegetable. And they've got the doctor on television testifying. The doctor who did this. And he's right there on TV saying he can't begin to say how sorry he is. Now there's nothing left for me to turn to.

I'm thinking of opening a bottle of brandy when this fantastic, redemptive piece of news comes on about a Chinese 747 which was on its way from China to L.A.; and all of the sudden it just drops out of the sky. It just starts to fall. It falls twenty-nine thousand feet just like that. It was only thirty seconds and a thousand feet away from plunging into the Pacific Ocean when the pilot suddenly brings it out of its plunge.

Now there is a man I'd like to meet—that pilot. And the words of one of those new-age positive thinkers come back to me. He's got a retreat in Hawaii, I forget his name. And he's always saying, "When you meet reality, you do one of three things: you fight it, you flee it, or you flow." And by "flow," I figure he means embrace your fears. That's how I interpret it. And that's a thought. That's the other side of paranoia, or the other side of antiparanoia. Somewhere in between. It's the middle way, to embrace the fear. That's what that pilot must have done with the last thousand feet. He must have put his arms around fear and gotten clear.

So I just turned off the TV and sat there and listened to the sound of the wind fill up the room. And I looked down at the brick hearth of the little fireplace that we couldn't use because the chimney needed cleaning. And all the smoke filled the room. And I looked down to see a copy of *Vanity Fair* with Diane Keaton dressed all in white smiling back. And then I looked up at the wall at this reproduction of this nineteenth-century painting of this ship sailing in a storm off the white cliffs of Dover. And that Matthew Arnold poem came back to me. That line. Through my head it went like a ticker tape. The line, you know, over and over was something like "Ah love, let us be true to one another. Ah love, let us be true." And I turned out the lights and watched the full moon as it flashed through the ripping palm trees and the spaces in the Venetian blind.

And I remembered that other rat—the one on Halloween back in New York City. By mistake I had cracked a shaving mirror and I was real upset because it was Halloween and I was afraid of seven years' bad luck. And then, when I was coming home at night, actually, coming to Renée's loft, which was one of many homes then, I was starting up the steps and I sensed kind of scrambling energy coming from under one of those steps in front of me. Now it's not as though I was not on the lookout for evil or death in those halls, but I had always expected it to take a human form—two big men coming at me with a knife. I just never expected it to be this. And out from under the seventh step, this huge brown city rat jumped onto my chest. And I fell back and let out with an involuntary yell. I just went "AHHHHHHH. . . ." And then I remembered the old saying "Never corner a rat" and I began running in circles so as not to corner him. And the rat must have heard the old saying about never corner a human being because it also ran in circles. And I was beating it with my raincoat. Beating it off, and we ran around and around till somehow the rat disappeared. It went away.

Now I knew I should have kept that whole event to myself. You know, just held on to it. I should have kept it as a secret—embraced my fear. You know, reprocess it, and not report it to Renée or any woman for that matter. You know, be like Christ. You know how Christ would take on evil stuff. He would take it on him, not pass it along. Like he had some sort of charcoal filter system in his psyche which enabled him to filter out evil karma or responses to it. Like a lobster. It's funny but I've always thought of Christ as a lobster. When I eat lobster I feel more like I'm eating the body of Christ because a lobster crawls on the bottom of the ocean and eats all this dead stuff, it eats garbage. It eats shit. And then it converts it all into this pure sweet white meat. And that's like Christ to me. He doesn't pass it on. And holding on to it doesn't cause cancer. Or maybe it would have if he had lived past thirty-three.

But the rat, I was telling you about the rat. Yes, I know where I was. Renée and the rat. Now I know how afraid of rats Renée was, and I could have just not told her what happened to me. You know, absorb it. Keep it to myself. But I didn't. When she called, I said, "Be careful when you come home because this big rat jumped out on my chest."

And she screamed and said, "That's it, I'm not coming home." And she hung up.

After about an hour or so, I hear this wild banging, and

it's Renée coming up the stairs with this big two-by-four. And she's swinging it and smashing the steps and walls and yelling. The rat was long gone by then.

But anyway, some demi-shaman friend of mine who lives upstate said that it would never happen twice. You know, to have a rat jump out on your chest would be like being hit by lightning twice. But the worst of it was that it made me paranoid and ill at ease. I thought it was a kind of black omen—I was sure it had to do with breaking the mirror on Halloween, and the rat was the beginning of seven years' bad luck. And I just didn't think I was ready for it. I was in no way ready for seven years' bad luck. So I came to Renée in the morning and I said, "Help me. What shall I do?"

And with all confidence and no thought about it, she said, "Kneel. Kneel down and kiss my grandmother Rivkala's ring."

This beautiful ring was the only thing that Renée's grandmother had left her. Her grandmother was poor and from Russia. Peasant stock. And she had left Renée this ring. And I wanted to believe in it. I wanted to believe in the power of the ring.

And Renée said, "Kiss the ring, and you'll dispel all bad luck."

And I went down on my knees on the kitchen floor and I kissed the ring. And as I did it, I saw a long bridge of toothless smiles—all Renée's relatives marching out over the world and back to Russia. I saw them standing, smiling in bending wheat fields. And I was relieved. A burden lifted from my mind. And I felt clear again. Something had transpired that I didn't understand, but I knew that the seven years' bad luck had been lifted, or counteracted by Rivkala's ring.

Thinking on this ring I felt sleepy now, and crept into bed with Renée, who was naked and asleep and smelling like horses in a stable. Breathing beside me like the Russian wheat field going down in the summer wind. And I tucked in beside her, and we fit together like spoons. Her warm flesh heaved to adjust to mine, as my belly fit into the curve of her back.

And for one brief instant, we were one as that nuclear wind tore at the palms and split the moon through the Venetian blinds. I closed my eyes to it and saw just before sleep, I saw the last images spin out like a wheel of life and death. All spinning and mixed together. I saw the sacrificial blonde, sprawled, broken in her leaking blood. I saw the wild green money spinning in the wind above her, and above that, high high up, a Chinese 747 was about to fall from the sky. And above all this shedding rays of silver light was that ring. Rivkala's ring. That blessed ring. And beyond that, black black, dark black. Oh dark dark dark, forever dark. We all go into the dark.

Notes

At The Acting Company's world-premiere performance of *Orchards*, given at The Krannert Center for the Performing Arts in Champaign-Urbana, Illinois, on September 19, 1985, the seven plays were staged in the order in which they appear in this book.

The plays were directed by Robert Falls.

Sets designed by Adrianne Lobel. Costumes designed by Laura Crow. Lights designed by Paul Gallo. Original music by Louis Rosen. Dramaturg: Anne Cattaneo. Assistant Director: Rob Bundy. Production Stage Manager: Maureen F. Gibson. Stage Manager: Susan B. Feltman.

The casts were as follows:

The Man in a Case by Wendy Wasserstein

BYELKINOV	Brian Reddy
VARINKA	Mariangela Pino

Vint by David Mamet

PORTER	Craig Bryant
COMMISSIONER PERSOLIN	Terrence Caza
ZVISDULIN	Joel F. Miller
KULAKEVITCH	Phil Meyer
NEDKUDOV	Kevin Jackson
PSIULIN	Aled Davies

Drowning by Maria Irene Fornes

PEA	Philip Goodwin
ROE	Anthony Powell
STEPHEN	Mark Moses

A Dopey Fairy Tale by Michael Weller

SMILE	Phil Meyer
FATHER BAKER	Terrence Caza
MOTHER BAKER	Susan Finch
CLARENCE	Craig Bryant
CHATTER (the dog)	Joel F. Miller
MAYOR	Kevin Jackson
MAGISTRATE	Anthony Powell
MINISTER	Mark Moses
FEMALE FROG	Wendy Brennan
MALE FROG	Brian Reddy
SAD PRINCESS GLADYS	Laura Brutsman

Eve of the Trial by Samm-Art Williams

MA LOLA	Susan Finch
LESTER SIMMONS	Brian Reddy
PEARL SIMMONS	Laura Brutsman
TATE	Joel F. Miller
ALEX BUSHKIN	Philip Goodwin
LILLY	Mariangela Pino
KITTY	Wendy Brennan

The Talking Dog by John Guare

F	Susan Finch
M	Mark Moses
HANG-GLIDER #1	Kevin Jackson
HANG-GLIDER #2	Phil Meyer

Rivkala's Ring by Spalding Gray

THE SPEAKER	Aled Davies

A NOTE ABOUT THE PLAYWRIGHTS

Maria Irene Fornes is the author of *Promenade*, *The Successful Life of 3*, *Fefu and Her Friends*, *The Danube*, *Mud*, *Sarita*, and *The Conduct of Life*, all of which earned her Obie Awards for writing. She is the recipient of a Guggenheim Fellowship, a Rockefeller Foundation grant, and an award from the American Academy and Institute of Arts and Letters.

Spalding Gray has performed his autobiographical monologues to acclaim throughout the United States—at the Goodman Theater (Chicago), the Mark Taper Forum (Los Angeles), the Walker Art Center (Minneapolis), the Performing Garage and the Mitzi E. Newhouse Theater at Lincoln Center (New York)—as well as in Europe, Canada, and Australia. His 1985 monologue *Swimming to Cambodia* (available in book form) is based on his experiences on the set of *The Killing Fields*, in which he made his motion picture debut. Six of his monologues are collected in the book *Sex and Death to the Age 14*.

John Guare's plays—which include *Gardenia*, *Lydie Breeze*, *Bosoms and Neglect*, *Rich and Famous*, and *The House of Blue Leaves*—have earned him an Award of Merit from the American Academy and Institute of Arts and Letters. He also wrote the screenplay for *Atlantic City* (which won him an Oscar nomination as well as the New York, Los Angeles, and National Film Critics Prize for Best Screenplay) and the book and lyrics for *Two Gentlemen of Verona* (winner of the New York Drama Critics' Circle Award and the Tony Award for Best Musical).

David Mamet was awarded the Pulitzer Prize in 1984 for his play *Glengarry Glen Ross*. He is also the author of *American Buffalo*, *Sexual Perversity in Chicago*, *The Duck Variations*, *Prairie du Chien*, and *The Shawl*, among other plays. His adaptation of Chekhov's *The Cherry Orchard* was produced at the Goodman Theater in Chicago in 1985. His screenplays include *The Postman Always Rings Twice* and *The Verdict*.

Wendy Wasserstein is the author of *Uncommon Women and Others, Isn't It Romantic, Tender Offer*, and other plays. For the PBS *Great Performances* series she has adapted *Uncommon Women and Others* and John Cheever's story "The Sorrows of Gin." She is the recipient of a Guggenheim Fellowship and a grant from the National Endowment for the Arts.

Michael Weller's plays include *Moonchildren, Split, Fishing, Loose Ends, The Ballad of Soapy Smith*, and, most recently, *Ghost on Fire*, which premiered at the La Jolla Playhouse in 1985. He is the author of the screenplays for *Hair* and *Ragtime*.

Samm-Art Williams's play *Home*, produced on Broadway, won the Outer Critics' Circle Award for Best Play and was nominated for a Tony Award in the category of Best Play in 1980. His other plays include *Eyes of the American, Welcome to Black River, Friends, Brass Birds Don't Sing, The Sixteenth Round*, and *A Love Play*. He has also written extensively for television, and collaborated on the book of Broadway's *Lena Horne: The Lady and Her Music*.